Better Homes and Gardens.

fireplace
design & decorating ideas

A **Better Homes and Gardens** Book
An Imprint of
HMH

Published by:
Houghton Mifflin Harcourt
Boston • New York
www.hmhbooks.com

For information about permission to reproduce selections from this book, write to Permissions, Houghton Mifflin Harcourt Publishing Company, 215 Park Avenue South, New York, New York 10003.

www.hmhbooks.com

Library of Congress Control Number available from the publisher upon request.
ISBN: 978-1-118-36010-1

Printed in the United States of America

DOR 10 9 8 7 6 5 4 3 2 1

4500431135

BETTER HOMES AND GARDENS® MAGAZINE
Gayle Goodson Butler
Executive Vice President, Creative Content Leader
Oma Blaise Ford
Executive Editor
Michael D. Belknap
Creative Director

BETTER HOMES AND GARDENS® FIREPLACE DESIGN & DECORATING IDEAS
Editor: Lacey Howard
Contributing Editor: Debra Wittrup
Contributing Designer: Gayle Schadendorf
Contributing Copy Editor: Paul Soucy
Contributing Photographers: Adam Albright, Kritsada Panichgul, Dean Schoeppner, Jay Wilde
Contributing Writer: Debra Steilen
Contributing Producer: Molly Reid Sinnett
Contributing Illustrator: Tom Rosborough
Cover Photographer: Michael Partenio

SPECIAL INTEREST MEDIA
Editorial Director: James D. Blume
Content Director, Home: Jill Waage
Deputy Content Director, Home: Karman Hotchkiss
Managing Editor: Doug Kouma
Art Director: Gene Rauch
Group Editor: Lacey Howard
Assistant Managing Editor: Jennifer Speer Ramundt
Business Director: Janice Croat

MEREDITH NATIONAL MEDIA GROUP
President: Tom Harty
Director, Operations and Business Development: Doug Olson

MEREDITH CORPORATION
Chairman and Chief Executive Officer: Stephen M. Lacy

HOUGHTON MIFFLIN HARCOURT
Vice President and Publisher: Natalie Chapman
Editorial Director: Cindy Kitchel
Acquisitions Editor: Pam Mourouzis
Managing Editor: Marina Padakis

Welcome

Are you looking for innovative ways to incorporate a fireplace into a home you own or one you are planning to buy or build? Does your fireplace simply need a fresh new face? Or does a complete overhaul come to mind? You've no doubt answered yes to one of these questions, and you've come to the right place.

Every page of this book brims with decorating and design ideas that can help you make any fireplace as practical and as beautiful as possible. So turn the page, and let's get started.

contents

parts of a fireplace

The hearth industry does not use a common set of terms for the exterior parts of a fireplace, although it does have standardized terminology for the inner workings. In this book, we use these terms to describe the exterior elements. See the glossary on page 186 for further definitions of each term.

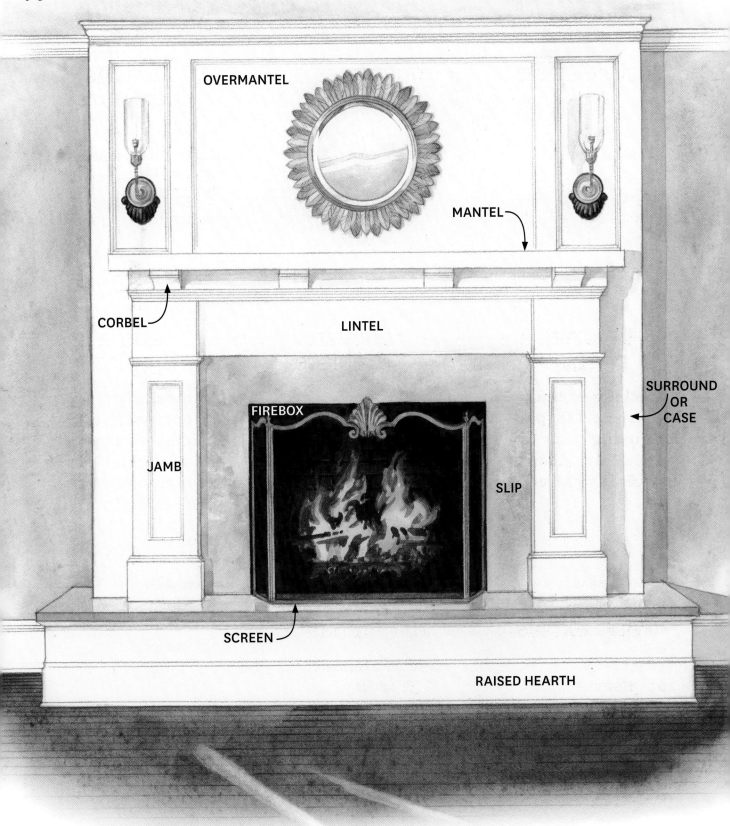

OVERMANTEL

MANTEL

CORBEL

LINTEL

SURROUND OR CASE

JAMB

FIREBOX

SLIP

SCREEN

RAISED HEARTH

style guide

As a focal point in any space, a fireplace can reflect your
home's architectural character or your decorating style.
In this chapter, you'll find fireplace designs that recall the
soaring hearths found in French châteaus, the rustic stone-
and-mortar style reminiscent of a woodland lodge, and the
symmetry and elegance associated with the finest classical
revivals. Whether you're building a new fireplace or
updating an existing hearth, use these inspirational images
to help you define the look for your room.

Old World

Re-create the look of the grand hearths that welcomed travelers, invited family gatherings, and warmed stately European homes as far back as the Middle Ages.

To fashion the old-world fireside look in your home, think big. In this time-tested style, hearths, mantels, overmantels, and surrounds are all weighty in appearance and large in scale compared with other fireplace styles.

Check with architectural salvage firms for antique stone fireplace surrounds, or look into cast-stone versions that mimic these more expensive materials. Whether you choose a piece that is prefabricated or cast on the spot, the finish can be glazed to look centuries old.

Balance the visual weight of the fireplace with surrounding materials, furnishings, and accents with heft or generous size. Use salvaged wood flooring or large-scale tiles, top walls with elaborate moldings, decorate with deep seating and sturdy tables, and choose fireplace screens and tools in heavy wrought iron, pewter, or copper.

OLD MEETS NEW *right* This family room has a strong Provençal feel thanks to an artful blending of old and new elements. The plaster wall finish is designed to match the patina of the natural limestone detailing on the substantial fireplace surround and overmantel.

IMPORTED LUXURY *opposite* A Louis XV reproduction bergère offers a place to relax in this master suite near an antique limestone fireplace imported from France. The curvaceous lines of the piece balance those of the chair. A beautiful trumeau mirror takes the French connection to the ceiling.

Old World

 FRENCH FINISH *opposite*
Monochrome but far from mundane, the stone fireplace and walls in this French-inspired family room share their mellowed texture with walnut armoires set into tailored niches. Furniture covered in cotton velvet has the same tone as the stonework, while shadowy grays and glimpses of black lend additional interest and structure.

LIGHT TOUCH
top Gilded iron candlesticks from Spain were converted into floor lamps that now flank this antique marble fireplace. An antique French trumeau mirror over the mantel adds substance to the small-scale hearth. Centered on the fireplace, a high pedestal table varies the levels of interest and leads the eye through the room.

EASY ELEGANCE
right Elegance comes easy in a room full of fine antiques, starting with a substantial limestone mantel plucked from a French chateau. Lined on the interior with narrow brick in classic French style, the firebox offers ample room for a dog grate and an elaborate cast iron fireback. Massive stone corbels support a deep mantel, the perfect spot to showcase collecting passions.

Old World

EXOTIC MIX *opposite* Uncluttered furnishings and an unfussy antique stone mantel enhance the feeling of openness in this living room that mixes Italian style with more exotic flavors: an elaborate Moroccan-inspired wood-panel ceiling and a sizable Moroccan mirror over the fireplace. Warm, rustic textures and a distinct lack of clutter create unpretentious beauty.

COUNTRY CASA *top left* A limestone mantel in this country casa living room showcases ornate candelabra and an antique Bible box. Statuesque child-size chairs, antique andirons, and a vintage tapestry enhance the room's gathered-over-time appeal. Off-white walls allow the individual pieces to shine.

CHATEAU STYLE *top center* Subtle shades of cream pick out the details on this remade fireplace fashioned after the Château de Groussay near Paris. A circular convex mirror and small ledges that display 18th- and 19th-century Delft jars are incorporated into ornate paneling above the mantel. Plaster fretwork on the ceiling continues the French-inspired decorative program through the room.

TUSCAN TONES *top right* Nestled into an arched recess, an oil painting enlivens the living room while drawing attention to the fireplace surround's two-tone pattern. A hefty case and overmantel pairs with intricate geometric motifs on the tile. Walls infused with amber tones infuse the room with Tuscan style.

SET IN STONE *right* Italian glass-and-gilded sconces from the 1940s and antique Louis XVI needlepoint chairs flank a dining room's 18th-century Louis XIV fireplace. A straightforward farm table with bench seating downplays the grandeur of the antique limestone structure. Walls designed to mimic plaster over stone and 14-foot-high vaulted ceilings lend European distinction.

Traditional

Inspired by the neoclassicism and fine cabinetmaking of the early republic, meticulously designed traditional fireplaces never go out of style.

Balance and order characterize the features of a traditional fireplace. Taking cues from the late 18th- and early 19th-century European and American interest in the decorative elements of ancient Greece, Rome, and Egypt, architectural details include crown moldings, finely crafted woodwork, lustrous and painted surfaces, and surrounds of polished marble, granite, or limestone.

A pleasing combination of gentle curves and rectilinear elements is often created by combining rounded columns or swagged wood or plaster appliques with geometric trim or pilasters.

Vintage accessories, including metal hardware, sconces, urns, framed prints, paintings or mirrors, and candlesticks, add instant age to a new fireplace built in a traditional style.

SIMPLY STUNNING *top* A beautifully rendered Adamesque design in white wood and black marble makes a stunning statement in an elegant bedroom. Simple fluted pilasters form the jambs, while an urn-and-swag motif decorates the lintel.

CLASSIC CARVING *right* Handcrafted scrollwork featuring high-relief foliage motifs frames a beautifully veined and polished marble surround. With its detailed decorative program and crisp paint finish, this hearth exemplifies the classically inspired traditional fireplace.

VICTORIAN VERVE *opposite* Original to the 150-year-old living room it graces, this wood and brick fireplace boasts fluted Ionic columns supporting plain corbels and a dentiled mantel shelf. Blue-and-white ceramics, gilded frames, and ornate andirons enrich the period look.

Traditional

FARM FRESH *above* Casework in unadorned stained wood and a flat black stone surround suit the fuss-free decor of this 1850s farmhouse living room. Pilasters topped with Doric-type capitals are the most decorative features of the hearth. Sage green cabinetry provides a soft contrast to the dark wood and stone.

OPEN WIDE *right* A striking contrast between the finely trimmed and painted wood case and the rustic river rock of the hearth surround creates a compelling focal point in this intimately scaled living room. The wide dimensions of the fireplace balance the staircase at the other end of the wall, while the strong horizontal lines embrace the cozy seating group.

timeline of architectural styles

A quick primer on traditional fireplace fashions from past centuries will tell you which styles were prevalent during your favorite decorative period.

- During the Tudor and Stuart reigns in Britain (1485–1688), fireplaces were grandly scaled with broad lintels spanning cavernous openings.

- In Colonial American homes (1600–1775), it was common to hang a large painting above the fireplace. Wall paneling framed the hearth like a showpiece.

- The Georgian period in Britain (1714–1837) saw fashionable Europeans ordering elaborately carved mantels and pairing them with marble slips. Classical designs—palmettes, scrolling acanthus leaves, and Ionic capitals—gave surrounds added grace.

- In the neoclassical period (1795–1850), designers looked to ancient Greece and Rome for detailed finery on carved wooden or marble surrounds, mantels, and overmantels.

- Victorians (1838–1901) had no fear of ornamentation and often took a Gothic turn, embracing medieval European traditions. Paneling, fretwork, and spindles all underscored the importance of the hearth in Victorian homes.

NEUTRAL BASE
above A wide surround makes this fireplace the dominant feature of a cozy family room. Neutral colors on walls and furnishings and the rich black marble slip bring the white-painted jambs and lintel into relief. Balanced above by matching wall sconces, the simple mantel arrangement ensures that focus remains on the linear elements of the white woodwork.

Traditional

BRICK WORKS
opposite Graceful moldings and paneled walls updated an original Cape Cod fireplace in this renovated 1960s ranch house. The brick surround brings warmth to the off-white walls.

TILE TALE *top left*
Thematically tied to the homeowner's collecting and outdoor passions, the blue-and-white tile slip sports images of sailing ships that echo the artwork over the mantel. Atop the chimneypiece and on adjoining bookcases, vintage weather vanes reinforce the Americana theme.

FRIEZE FRAME
top right
Neoclassical motifs such as egg-and-dart, dentil, swag, and palmette enliven this lintel carving.

WELL STUDIED
right This newly constructed fireplace looks like it was salvaged from a Greek Revival plantation house. The homeowners consulted period pattern books for an authentic look.

regional influence
Add a touch of local flavor.

Southwest. A smooth adobe-like finish in earth-inspired hues or a surround of colorful glazed tiles lends a Southwestern look.

Mountain lodge. A fireplace of rugged unpolished stone with a rustic wood mantel and a raised hearth suggests the snug comfort and relaxed ways of vacation hideaways.

Cape Cod. More refined than the lodge look, these hearths use indigenous material, from smooth woods to heavily textured stones, to fashion nature-inspired beauty in earthy colors.

Country

Snug and simply furnished, country style is an American legacy that is as well-suited to urban high-rises and suburban ranches as it is to log cabins and clapboard Colonials.

Country style can be rustic or refined, but it always invites people to gather at the hearth.

Whether you're looking for a casual or a sophisticated country look, keep the millwork simple: A shallow mantel adorned with simple accessories creates an understated background. For an even more authentic early American look, install a vintage painted mantel over a firebox made from salvaged bricks, or cover the mantel wall with paneling, evoking images of early American homes. Add classical elements, such as a keystone at the peak of an arched slip or fluted pilasters on the jambs, for a more formal look.

Millwork in casual country is often stockier with fewer refinements, and fireplace surrounds are sometimes of rough masonry to give the look of stone harvested from nearby fields.

GET COOKING
right Made from native Arkansas stone, this fireplace is designed for cooking and heating. The raised hearth makes it comfortable to cook over the flames and provides storage niches beneath for supplies. A swing arm holds cast-iron pots for simmering soups and stews.

COLOR CUES
opposite Salvaged from a nearby vacant lot, a black-painted cypress mantel grounds the arrangement in this New Orleans living room. Embraced by wainscoting in a rich terra-cotta hue, the dark hearth balances the bright aqua ceiling color.

Country

far left **PLAIN & SIMPLE** *far left* A dining room fireplace in an 1850s Maryland farmhouse takes on European flavor with the addition of an 18th-century French monastery table. Drop cloths made into chair skirts and a plain linen table runner echo the pastoral simplicity of the unadorned fireplace.

WARM WELCOME *top* A cozy palette makes this family room glow. A sectional sofa, covered in large-scale yellow-and-cream checks, anchors the seating arrangement around a floor-to-ceiling fieldstone fireplace that exudes warmth even when it's not lit. The overmantel accommodates a TV to signal that this room is meant for kick-back comfort.

TONAL TEXTURE *bottom* This living area focuses on a soaring stone fireplace and a wall of shelves showcasing a collection of circular objects. The neutral palette places a premium on the texture and quiet interplay of subdued hues supplied by the rough stone.

adding vintage elements
Add instant age with architectural salvage.

Vintage doesn't come in standard sizes. When looking for an antique mantel to pair with an existing firebox, bring along exact measurements of the height and width of the box and the fireplace wall.

Scale matters when pairing a vintage piece with a new fireplace. Keep overall dimensions in scale with the room's size and height. You can achieve a stylish look by using a fireplace that is oversized or deliberately small, but be sure it conveys a decorative choice, not an aesthetic blunder.

Country

MOUNTAIN VIEW *opposite* As monumental as the mountains outside, this massive stone fireplace and rustic wood-beam mantel anchor a warm family room. Comfy leather chairs and a cheery painting above provide the homey touches that allow the fireplace to enhance rather than overwhelm.

TWO-FACED *above* This open brick fireplace shows its rustic and refined versatility indoors and out.

HOME FIRES *right* Original to this 1778 farmhouse kitchen, the fireplace looks at home in the updated room sited next to a modern refrigerator housed in a handsome armoirelike cabinet.

And they lived happily ever after

cottage style

Add a touch of romance to your country look.

The appealing mix of comfort, simplicity, and nostalgia in American country style also marks the interiors of many beachside cottages. But the lines are softer than country, and the furnishings are rounder.

Mimic the softer look in the hearth with smooth finishes or curvy lines. The mantra of cottage is "comfort and ease"; the mantel and surround of a cottage-style hearth should convey the same breezy attitude.

Arts and Crafts

At the end of the 19th century, the excesses and industrialism of the Victorian era triggered a return to the simple virtues of handcrafted interiors.

Simplicity is the watchword of Arts and Crafts style. After the gilded flourishes of the previous 50 years, a snug bungalow or plain foursquare with austere finishes and trimwork became the order of the day. The solid woodwork and strong rectilinear elements of Craftsman and Mission styles exemplify the Arts and Crafts aesthetic.

To give your fireside Arts and Crafts appeal, use a palette of cream, terra-cotta, earthy brown, and sage green. Keep the mantel and hearth design boldly simple, with square corners and a few sturdy flourishes. Tile and brick facades with plank wood mantels create the desired geometric design and solid feel. A frame of posts and beams defining the fireplace setting is another signature Arts and Crafts detail.

Choose furnishings with no-nonsense lines. Use sturdy fabrics, hammered or matte metals, and matte-finish pottery.

ARTISTIC EDGE *top right* Handcrafted finishes, artisanal touches, and quality craftsmanship were hallmarks of the Arts and Crafts sensibility. The exquisite inlay and carving seen on this chimneypiece as well as the fine materials show off the style to its best advantage.

FUSS-FREE FIRE *right* Grained wood on the mantel and jambs, a stone slab lintel, and a stone-tiled slip give this fireplace character without a lot of decorative excess. Although lower than normal for turn-of-the-century bungalows, the built-in cabinets on either side of the hearth are typical of Arts and Crafts design. The zebra-print chair adds a bit of modern-day flair.

WARM FINISH This simply designed mantel features the solid woodwork used throughout the home. Part of a large, unobstructed room tied to a renovated kitchen, the mantel stain provided the cue for the kitchen cabinets.

Arts and Crafts

ON THE PRAIRIE *opposite* Mixing Colonial tastes with Prairie-style proportions, this wide fireplace embraces the many faces of Arts and Crafts style. The encaustic artwork over the mantel emphasizes the broad structure.

NICE NICHE *top right* Clinker bricks form the raised hearth, surround, and stepped mantel on this master bedroom fireplace. To balance the entry door on the right, a walk-in closet was added to the left of the hearth, creating a niche that enclosed the fireplace. Thanks to its depth, symmetrical placement, and antique doors, it looks original.

NOOK LOOK *center right* Mantel-height wainscoting on the walls and a wing-back style enclosure form a bench seat. Paired with a matching seat on the opposite side of the arched brick fireplace, they form a classic inglenook, often found in early 20th-century bungalows.

LOCAL FLAVOR *right* Stones excavated from the property went into this living room fireplace. All the timber used—in beams, columns, exposed rafters, and interior walls—was harvested within 30 miles of the house. An earthy color palette connects the room to its woodsy location.

inglenooks
Built-in seating creates the perfect spot for fireside reading or relaxing.

In its purest form, the inglenook is distinctly set off, a sort of room within a room. The hearth is tucked into its own cozy space, then it is flanked with built-in seating, *left*.

One way to do this is by building a raised platform so that you step up to the fireplace seating area. Another is to lower the ceiling to differentiate the hearth area from the main portion of the room. Or build half-walls or bookcases to enclose the inglenook space.

The twin benches of many inglenooks face each other at right angles to the hearth. This arrangement gives the best view of the fire, but seating built along the fireplace wall is another option. A raised hearth often incorporates a broad ledge that forms just such a seating spot.

Contemporary

Sleek and simple surfaces and plain geometry became the prevalent style direction in 1930s Art Deco and continued through 1950s modern.

Contemporary style incorporates a wide range of design influences, from machine-age streamlining through eco-friendly ergonomics. Opt for a no-frills fireplace with clean lines and subtle contours that will repeat in the room's decor. Create this cosmopolitan look by paring your room down. Bare floors, minimal window treatments, and exposed construction elements such as ceiling trusses, ductwork, or fireplace flues set the stage.

Consider flat-front cabinets in a light, subtly grained wood such as ash, birch, or maple, or opt for a flat, natural tile surround. For extra shine, choose a polished black granite slip or a curved glass fire screen.

Bring a homey touch with colors and materials as warm and welcoming as they are clean-lined. Natural or lightly stained honey-tone and red woods are good choices for mantels and casework.

NOW AND THEN *top* Original to this 1957 *Better Homes and Gardens* Idea Home, the architecture of the living room was kept intact by the new owners. They painted the fireplace a slate gray to draw attention to it and to the vaulted ceiling.

FEELING BLUE *right* Quietly unobtrusive, this painted brick fireplace could easily have faded into the background of the living room. With a bright hue of aqua, however, the overmantel becomes a focal point in the space and surrounds a favorite work of art. The wide mantel shelf runs the length of the wall, embracing both the fireplace and the shelves of collected vessels on either side.

A gorgeous stone
surround and mantel
like this can live
indoors or out. The
stunningly simple
play of two colors
and materials makes
a strong design
statement. Topped
by a unique mirror
and flanked by two
porch swing sofas,
this hearth takes
center stage.

Contemporary

Warm a contemporary room with a generous helping of natural light and touch-me textures such as soft leather.

BOXED IN *above* A plain gas-burning firebox set into this family room wall is all that's needed for a cozy fireplace. Salvaged wood beams above and below the box provide the visual structure. Built-in shelving overhead showcases collectibles and acts as the overmantel for the contemporary hearth.

BLACK HOLES *opposite* Pairing the twin focal points of a large-screen TV and a fireplace, this white-painted brick structure provides the anchor and function for this family room. Classic modern furnishings, such as the gray upholstered Arne Jacobsen Egg Chairs, reinforce the contemporary vibe of a room that sanctions the marriage of traditional hearth and high-tech electronics.

Contemporary

HIT THE HEIGHTS Flooded with natural light, this new fireplace looks original to the house thanks to its geometric design, grand scale, and craggy stone face.

industrial chic

To fashion a look with a raw edge, consider the beauty of this unique and eco-friendly style.

If you'd like to bring some factory chic into your rooms, opt for exposed pipes and ductwork, open ceilings, and salvaged woods, fixtures, furnishings, and architectural parts. Repurpose rusty gears as functional handles or as an object of interest on the mantel. An added benefit: The reused materials are durable and low-maintenance.

This doesn't mean that you have to live in a former factory warehouse or open loft to get the look. In these suburban rooms, the owners have brought in a touch of industrial chic.

Sleek unadorned slabs of limestone form the lintel and jambs of this simple fireplace, *right*. A raised hearth of limestone runs along the fireplace wall to provide seating, display space, and storage for wood and tools.

A plain concrete-outlined inset gas fireplace, *bottom right,* floats in the wall beneath a raw reclaimed wood beam that fashions a wide mantel for a series of collectible artwork. The hard lines of the wood and concrete are softened by cushy curvy orange chairs and an ottoman side table.

Pine-clad walls and ceiling create a warm, casual mood that balances the clean design of this fireplace, *below*. Factory-style pendant lights float in the large open space.

Transitional

First called 'eclectic' to describe the jumble of styles prevalent in the early 20th century, the term morphed into what we now call transitional, the blending of old and new, traditional and modern.

"If you like it, you can make it work" is the common mantra for this kind of interior design. Mixing and matching architecture, furnishings, and fixtures from different periods results in a transitional-style room. Appealing but hard-to-categorize fireplaces can create a decorating challenge, as can a traditional-style fireplace in a room of modern decor.

If your fireplace seems out of sync with your decorating style, then coax it into compliance. A monochromatic color scheme can quickly incorporate an out-of-place fireplace and blend it with your furnishings.

Use motifs found in your fireplace as a theme or embrace contrasts between hearth and decor by playing off differences in scale, color, or shape.

Consider your choice of materials as a source of unity, too. Choose matching or harmonizing wood tones or stone types.

DUAL PERSONALITY
right A fieldstone fireplace wears two faces: On the dining room side, it's distinctly country, providing a textural and tonal backdrop to collected and unique furnishings. On the living room side, its character tends toward contemporary, its flat and simple structure complementing the group of matched chairs and glass coffee table.

PAINT POWER
opposite A simple palette demonstrates the power of paint, creating a natural backdrop for a Spanish Colonial Revival-style fireplace and the modern wingback chairs and furnishings.

room divider

Divide and conquer your open spaces with a fireplace wall.

Choose the size. Broad or narrow, half-height or ceiling height, the wall will create a dividing line for activities, direct traffic flow, and regulate light.

Mind your materials. When designing a divider, take your cues from the style of the existing room. Pay careful attention to the materials used and the scale of all the elements that make up the fireplace wall.

Transitional

INSPIRING ART *opposite* Broad swaths of white paint lighten the feel of this traditional surround and overmantel. The painting above provides the color scheme for the room and ties the fireplace to the mix of found and slipcovered furnishings.

ECLECTIC ELEGANCE *top left* Parsons tables, tub chairs, and an antique velvet bergère surround a unique Rookwood tile fireplace. Antiqued mirrors hide bookshelves on either side.

FOR THE BIRDS *top right* This fireplace wall becomes a focal point with a large Audubon-inspired print. Instead of one gigantic mirror above, appropriate-scale, curvier alternatives on a soft aqua wall flank the mantel.

SLEEK AND SIMPLE *center, far left* A large modern painting, substantial crown moldings, and an all-white palette make more of a simple hearth in an old home. A decorative grate and marble slip create a pleasing contrast with sleek furnishings.

MODERN BALANCE *center left* A plain stone surround and an unadorned narrow mantel bring a contemporary sensibility to a traditionally styled room. A balanced arrangement of artwork fills the wall around the hearth, echoed by the symmetrical grouping of furnishings.

QUIET BEAUTY *far left* An antique stone fireplace in an old house gives an open sunroom gravitas and simplicity. Modern furnishings, bluestone pavers, and a neutral palette help to lighten the mood in a room made for family gatherings.

MIDCENTURY REVIVAL *left* Reclaimed from a 1950s Colonial, a traditional surround gets a second life in a whole-house renovation. A granite slip adds warmth, while millwork details seamlessly integrate into the paneling on the adjoining walls.

room
by room

Over the past 150 years, fireplaces have gone from necessity to luxury. In the days before central heating, a fireplace in the bedroom was the only way to stave off winter's chill. Today, a bedroom fireplace offers a touch of romance, while one in a dining room provides a hint of splendor. Enticing in a master bath or on a patio, a fireplace should be considered for any remodel or addition. Page through our room-by-room guide to see how a fireplace can introduce a cozy and dreamy quality to any space in your home.

Living Rooms

Designed for togetherness, living rooms, family rooms, and great-rooms offer perfect spaces for the warmth and welcome of a glowing fire.

A fireplace immediately adds comfort and character to any room, and it cues family and friends to the room's personality. A stately, formal fireplace sets the living room apart as a spot for special occasions. In the family room or great-room, a casual fireplace of rustic stone signals everyone to relax and unwind. Add a TV over the mantel or to the side, and the fireplace becomes the center of an evening's entertainment.

In any living space, set off the hearth by finishing it in a color that contrasts with the walls. Top a mantel with oversize artwork or draw attention to the firebox with custom-made doors or a hand-forged screen. Raise the hearth 12 to 18 inches off the floor to give it more prominence and provide seating.

Group chairs or sofas close to the fireplace and define the gathering spot with an area rug. Leave space between the fireplace and furnishings for safety.

WOODED BLISS *top* Warm woods in natural and sage green tones on the wall and surround call to mind a walk in a fall forest, a feeling reiterated by the artwork above the mantel. Furthering the sense of warmth, cushy upholstered seating clusters around the amply sized firebox.

CLEAN AND QUIET *right* Everything about this living room breathes elegance and simplicity. Balanced arrangements of seating, window treatments, and lighting, along with a limited and neutral color palette, project a character of formality onto this plain and straitlaced fireplace.

POINT BREAK
A stone hearth and towering chimney dominate and set the character for this formal and clean-lined living room, dividing it physically and visually from the more casual patio on the other side.

Living Rooms

SHAPE SHIFTER *above* The unusual Gothic design of the arched slip sets this fireplace apart and makes it stand out from the matching white walls. The tone-on-tone effect invites further inspection and reveals additional details such as the broken mantel entablature and the brickwork of the arch. Lines and shapes echo around the room on upholstery, pillows, the rug, and the drum coffee tables.

BURST OF ENERGY *right* Formality reigns supreme in this elegant living room. Symmetrically placed cabinets, glass vases, and sofas surround a floor-to-ceiling hearth of textural brick that encapsulates the room's color scheme within its material. A unique take on the classic sunburst mirror over the simple mantel adds energy and acts as a foil to all the linear elements in the room.

making your hearth cozy

Installing a fireplace is the first step to adding ambiance to your living space. Try these ideas to ensure the hearth becomes a favorite family gathering spot.

- Keep a supply of warm and nubby throws nearby for snuggling on chilly evenings. Add down-filled pillows to seating for sink-in comfort.

- Use natural textures such as woven baskets, wool, cotton, or linen textiles, unpolished stone, and rough wood.

- Display personal collections on the mantel, a raised hearth, or a nearby table. Group items for visual effect, and refresh the display frequently.

- If you don't have the luxury of built-in bookcases near your fireplace, keep a stack of books on a side table next to hearthside seating. Nothing is more relaxing than reading by the fire.

- Put lamps on dimmer switches to regulate light levels easily. Bring in more coziness with candlelight. Group pillar candles on the mantel or on sidetables and light them when entertaining.

- Use flexible furnishings that can serve double duty depending on your needs. Select ottomans that can also serve as coffee tables or a console table that can act as an impromptu buffet in a pinch.

ARTISTIC ECHO *above left* Soft colors and simple shapes ensure that the fireplace remains the focal point of this balanced room arrangement. Artwork above the mantel draws the eye and echoes the small, vertically oriented firebox below.

MURAL MATE *top right* Everything about this fireplace commands attention. Above the beautifully trimmed mantel, the TV takes the place of artwork between two large sconces. The colors of the marble slip and blue ceramics atop the mantel complement the wall mural that hugs the hearth on the right.

BLENDED SURROUNDINGS *above right* Painting the case of the fireplace to match the room's trim puts most of the focus on the pretty tile slip and the decorative insert. The heavy and dark wood cabinet next to the hearth provides visual balance.

Living Rooms

STONE STACK

opposite The rugged texture of this dry-stacked stone fireplace provides contrast to the smooth finishes elsewhere in this cottage living room. Keeping the mantel empty puts the focus on the variations found within the rustic material.

EVEN HANDED

top left Built-ins on either side of the fireplace lend a note of architectural symmetry to this room while providing practical storage and display space.

COMFY CLUBS

top right Keep furnishings around a family room fireplace casual. These leather club chairs and deep sofa offer durable comfort.

HIT THE HEIGHTS *right* Raising the height of the hearth places the flames near eye level for guests seated in the side chairs flanking this fireplace. An ornate stone lintel makes the chimneypiece a prominent feature of the room.

Dining Rooms

Light a fire in the dining room hearth, and without speaking a word, you've invited guests to linger long after the table is cleared.

A fireplace in the dining room contributes to a relaxed and gracious meal. It embraces a gathering of friends sitting around the table for an evening of laughter and good conversation warmed by the light of flickering flames.

The fireplace in a rectangular dining room is best sited on a long wall with the dining table parallel to it. If space is available, a raised hearth will bring the fireplace opening up to eye level for most guests seated at the table. Keep comfort and safety in mind: If you seat diners too close to the fireplace, the heat may be overwhelming.

Play down the perceived formality of a dining room by introducing asymmetrical arrangements of casual furnishings and personal objects or artwork on the mantel. Mix and match chairs and tableware and drape upright chairs with loose-fitting slipcovers.

COLOR FOCUS *right* **Striking** abstract art and bookshelf backs painted in sharply contrasting gray surround a white-painted fireplace with drama. Simple furnishings in the room and uncluttered displays keep the focus on the fireplace wall.

MODERN CLASSIC *opposite* Classical elements in this dining room, such as the carved chimneypiece, sunburst mirror above the mantel, paired candlesticks, and elaborate moldings, suggest a formal and traditional setting. Contemporary furnishings with gleaming surfaces make it a thoroughly modern one.

Dining Rooms

BARELY THERE

opposite Fascinating figures frolic on the tile slip of this imposing fireplace. A set of Philippe Starck Louis Ghost Chairs downplays the formality of this symmetrically arranged room and gives the patterned rug a chance to shine.

WHITE WASH

right White walls, cabinets, and dining chair slipcovers make a feature of the rustic brick fireplace facade and small mantel. A pastoral scene in the painting above reinforces the room's traditional character.

TASTE TEST

below An insert between wine cabinets raises the firebox to viewing level for diners. A mix of dark, light, and ebony woods and white walls and trim keep the decor simple, placing all the emphasis on the dining or wine-tasting experience.

Complement your cuisine with a dining room fireplace, and watch family and guests warm up to mealtime.

Dining Rooms

SCALE DOWN
The domestic scale of the fireplace surround keeps this dining room, with its soaring ceiling, massive beams, and bank of French doors, more intimate than imposing.

AGE APPROPRIATE *above* A salvaged antique fireplace surround brings instant character to this dining room. Peeling paint and a plain brick slip tie in well with the Shaker-style table and chairs.

COUNTER WEIGHT *right* An ornate surround of multihued marble gives this fireplace the design weight to balance the high ceilings, artwork, and arching bookcase.

STAND-OUT STRUCTURE *below left* Although tucked into a corner, this fireplace is no wallflower. The broad mantel shelf and lithic structure prevent the hearth from blending into the surrounding wall.

TRIPLE PLAY *below right* This dining room wears many hats as a library and work space. The unadorned fireplace allows the room to take on any role it needs to play, from hosting a sit-down dinner to poring over an illustrated volume, to paying bills.

Kitchens

Once upon a time, every kitchen had a fireplace as the center of the home's activity. Encourage that cozy feeling with a fireplace in your kitchen.

Although living rooms tend to get the most attention when it comes to fireplaces, let's face it: The kitchen is where people usually gather for companionship. So it makes sense to add a fireplace where friends and family can really enjoy its warmth and beauty.

But just like other features, a fireplace needs to complement your kitchen's style—especially if the space is open to adjacent rooms. For an old-world or country-style interior, consider a fireplace surround built from flagstone, brick, or terra-cotta tile. Add additional elegance to a classic traditional kitchen with a carved limestone surround or a wood one—stained or painted— embellished with layers of millwork. An Arts and Crafts-style space calls for a fireplace surround of glazed ceramic tiles or quartersawn oak. Stainless-steel, concrete, and slabs of granite or marble suit a contemporary kitchen.

OLD-WORLD APPEAL *top* With its imposing limestone surround, this fireplace fits right in with the kitchen's Tuscan personality. A mantel display of olive oil jugs celebrates the flavors of Italy.

VINTAGE ATTRACTION *right* Rough stone forms the hearth, firebox, and mantel, giving them a centuries-old look that complements the furniture's distressed surfaces.

PARTY TIME *opposite* Flanked by integrated refrigerators, a fireplace turns the kitchen into an entertaining zone. Gathering at the island becomes an opportunity to socialize with the chef while waiting for dinner.

Kitchens

hearth & home

Check out these practical tips for your kitchen's fireplace.

Vision quest.
Install a kitchen hearth at eye level for seated diners. The glow of firelight turns casual meals into special occasions.

Safe zone.
Allow enough space around the fireplace so that seating and traffic don't create safety hazards.

Flavor fest.
Expand your pizza- and bread-making abilities by opting for a wood-burning oven in place of a traditional fireplace. But make sure you include a generous ledge as a landing spot for hot dishes.

CONTEMPORARY CHIC *left* A monumental stained-concrete surround gives this fireplace a quiet drama in a great-room filled with glass, gleaming metal, and shiny finishes. An exposed chimney with stainless-steel accents and a floating display shelf add interest without drawing attention away from the kitchen's showstopping island.

CORNER VIEW *top* An angled installation guarantees this fireplace is visible from all corners of the room. A keystone arch gives the surround an old-world feel that complements other surfaces.

TRADITIONAL ELEGANCE *above* Magnificent corbels and a dramatic mantel make this fireplace a focal-point attraction. The hearth sits above deep storage drawers that hold pots, pans, and bakeware.

Bedrooms

You don't put a fireplace in the bedroom because you want to make popcorn. It's about what a hearth can do to enhance the room's style, as well as its capacity for rest, relaxation, and romance.

The addition of a fireplace should boost your bedroom's comfort quotient. Design your floor plan for pleasure. Angle the bed to provide the best possible view of the fireplace. If there's room, add one or two comfy chairs or a cozy love seat facing the hearth for flame-kissed fireside reading. Adorn the mantel area with accents you'll enjoy gazing at from bed: a favorite painting, a pottery collection, or beautifully framed photos of family and friends. Make sure there's a plush rug on the floor between bed and hearth—in the event you have to get up to toss another log on the fire.

On a practical note: There's no denying the sigh-inducing scent and sounds of a crackling, wood-burning fire. But the truth is you'll be more likely to use your fireplace if it's a gas-powered model you can control with a remote from under the covers. No stoking required.

FOCAL-POINT PLAN *right* Every piece in this soothingly neutral room radiates out from the fireplace's central location: the four-poster bed, the armchair and ottoman, and the matching pair of dressers. A formal arrangement tops the mantel over the Boston fern, a fair-weather substitute for a blaze.

GALLERY VIEW *opposite* This bed provides the best seat in the house—offering a close, personal view of the minimalist white fireplace and a few choice pieces of art. Bookshelves and drawers add function and storage while keeping the focus on the flames.

Bedrooms

GRACIOUS LIVING *right* White-painted woodwork provides a crisp counterpoint to soothing mauve walls and textiles in this elegant boudoir. The surround's architectural embellishments and the diamond-pattern fireplace screen offer a stylish foundation for the intricately carved mirror frame above.

EDWARDIAN ELEGANCE *below* The curved silhouette of a carved limestone fireplace highlights an ultra-feminine bedroom styled to soothe. Amidst a host of pinks and creams, the four-poster bed is placed to face both the fireplace and a large, arched window.

PRETTY IN PASTELS *far right* Decorative ceramic tiles give a sedate fireplace a scheme that complements the room's fresh furnishings. On the mantel, a gilt-framed mirror takes the place of a window, delivering a beautiful view of the room and its ornate chandelier. Twin yellow armchairs glow against the serene background, offering an intimate setting for a fireside chat.

Bedrooms

WHITE SPACE
Timelessly tranquil, a white fireplace surround combined with red bricks and white walls leaves plenty of room for personal expression. Blue-and-white-striped rugs and other textiles add a nautical note. And on the mantel, a tall piece of framed art takes the eye all the way up to the ceiling.

DYNAMIC DUO *above* With its Greek-inspired columns, this stone fireplace provides a handsome complement to the room's lush furnishings.

BIG DIVIDE *right* Placed between the bedroom and bath, this floor-to-ceiling fireplace brings warmth to both spaces simultaneously.

SPACE AGE *far right, center* An exposed chimney allows this hearth to float in midair, perfectly suited to the sleek space it occupies.

CHARM CLASS *far right* A masculine fireplace sets the tone for the entire bedroom with its elegant wood surround and slate slip.

Bathrooms

Soul-soothing and style-setting: These qualities go hand-in-hand when a fireplace is nestled into a well-appointed master bath.

A fireplace in the bath appeals to your soul's longing for beauty. Use luxurious materials you can enjoy viewing and touching. Frame the firebox in layers of polished or tumbled stone, glazed tiles, or painted wood that suit the suite. Add a decorative fire screen and handsome andirons. Adorn the mantel with collectibles that stand up to humidity. Move in a comfy chair for snuggling, since chances are you'll want to linger long past the time when the bath is done.

Design the layout so the tub faces the flames, or position it parallel to the fireplace to soak in the most heat. Consider a double-sided fireplace that can warm the bathroom and bedroom at the same time. It's all about creating a private retreat that sets a mood you and your partner can enjoy.

STREAMLINED STYLE *top right* With a double-sided fireplace that vents through the ceiling, both the bathroom and bedroom can be heated simultaneously. On the bathroom side, using the same mosaic tile for the fireplace wall and the tub unifies the space for a clean, contemporary look.

ARTISTIC IMPACT *right* Raising the marble hearth 18 inches off the floor gives bathers a clear view of this fireplace as they relax in the tub. The striking silver-trimmed screen mimics the undressed muntin windows.

VERDANT VIEW *opposite* In a room filled with decorative art, the fireplace remains a focal point thanks to its glossy green subway-tile slip and hearth. White-painted woodwork pairs a mirrored shelf with glass-front cabinet doors to display favorite collectibles. A white cast-iron lion guards the whole arrangement.

Bathrooms

LAYERS OF LUXURY *opposite* An elegant gray-and-white color scheme culminates in a fireplace with a marble slip and a white-painted mantel festooned with architectural trim. A polished-nickel screen visually links the fireplace to other fixtures: tub filler, faucets, lighting, mirrors, and the tub's elaborate claw feet.

TILE TREATMENT *top left* With walls, floor, and even the tub surround covered with lustrous mosaic tile, the black metal frame of the firebox turns the unit into a work of art.

CENTER OF ATTENTION *above* In this spacious master bath, a corner installation gives the massive fireplace a place of honor. Such recognition is well deserved, given the unit's limestone surround and arched fireplace screen reminiscent of decorative iron gates.

STARK STYLING *center, far left* High-contrast materials give this master bath a sophisticated contemporary presence. The rectangular black fireplace surround echoes the look of the tub's decorative legs as well as the freestanding storage tower.

CHIC SOLITUDE *center left* Clearly this master bath is all about the bathing experience. The head of the tub faces a fireplace wall, where an arched firebox contains flames behind a distinctive fire screen. Hanging above is gilt-framed artwork, and to the right, a large window overlooks lush landscaping.

RELAXATION STATION *left* Matching red leather chairs punctuate the indulgent nature of a fireplace that warms both a conversation area and a large soaking tub amid a sea of marble. The architecturally elegant mantel adds a sophisticated touch with its artful grouping of framed prints and a vase of tree branches arched just so.

Outdoors

Install a fireplace outside, and you instantly extend your living space and the amount of time you can spend enjoying the environment.

If your home includes a porch, patio, or sunroom, chances are these spaces are only enjoyed on nice days. What's missing? A source of heat that encourages alfresco dining and entertaining.

Enter the outdoor fireplace. It encourages folks to stay a little longer and gather closer to the flames.

Stylistically, it may make sense to tie a fireplace design into your home's exterior, matching materials and architectural details. Or create a fireplace organically connected to the landscape. Either way, enhance traffic flow by building the outdoor fireplace within easy access of the rooms in which you normally entertain.

Furnish your fireside room with a sturdy table and chairs if being used for dining, or use lightweight lounge seating that can be moved closer to or farther away from the flames as needed.

HOME STYLE
right Located close to French doors that open to a great-room, this fireplace, table, and chairs help extend the area that can be used for entertaining. The fireplace's limestone facade blends seamlessly into the home's flagstone exterior. A candle-powered chandelier brings a note of romance.

SECLUDED SETTING *opposite*
Marking the boundary between the private courtyard and landscape, this towering stucco fireplace becomes a relaxation destination. A "floor" of pea gravel adds texture underfoot while terra-cotta pots offer spots of color.

Outdoors

LIKE HOME
opposite In a setting suited to all conditions—with an overhang to protect against inclement weather and easy access to the stars after the sun goes down—comfortable seating encourages guests to linger near the concrete-edged fireplace.

SET ON STONE
top This massive fireplace anchors a courtyard that includes a seating area and an outdoor kitchen. Matching stone anchors the pergola, the gas grill, and assorted flower beds.

GARDEN FRESH
center right The ultimate in alfresco dining, this table and chairs are set close to the fireplace—but allow enough room that guests enjoy the view without being bothered by the BTUs.

CORNER ACTION *center, far right* An enormous terra-cotta chiminea guards the corner of this patio, offering a monolithic presence during the day and a source of heat in the evening air.

TILE DECOR
right Built into a flagstone chimney, this fireplace shows that decorative tiles needn't be reserved for indoor use. They brighten this fireplace slip and echo floral accents around the patio.

portable fireplaces
Need a quick fix of flames? Consider these two options when choosing a freestanding source of heat.

Fire pits. Because they're generally round or square, low-standing fire pits can be enjoyed equally from all sides. These metal substitutes for campfires suit large yards with multiple seating areas. Look for sturdy models that resist tipping.

Chimineas. Originally made of fired clay, chimineas (which resemble miniature pot-belly stoves with front-load openings) also come with cast-metal construction. More interesting when viewed from the front, chimineas suit smaller spaces when stationed on the sidelines. Place a patio block or hearth pad beneath a chiminea if using it on a wood deck.

arrange
furniture

Make your room work with furniture choices and placement that make the most of your fireplace. In this chapter, you'll learn ways to arrange furniture in a variety of situations: serene symmetrical rooms with centered fireplaces; large open spaces teeming with activity; rooms with breathtaking views that compete with the hearth; and out-of-the-ordinary rooms that demand unique ideas. Learn how to finesse your fireside groupings by using built-ins, managing traffic flow, and properly dealing with that all-important electronic hearth: the television.

Symmetry

When carried through to the tiniest detail, a symmetrical furniture arrangement creates a serene feeling of balance and order.

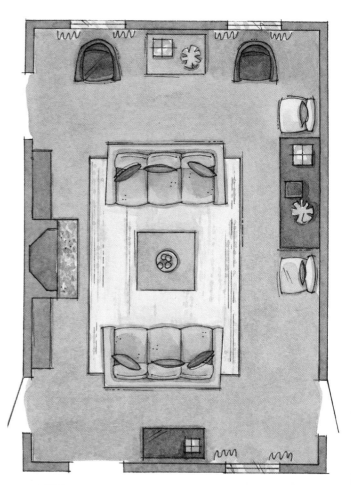

Start the design process by looking at your room's architectural bones. Is your fireplace flanked by matching windows or identical bookcases? If so, you may have found your inspiration, because such symmetry is instantly appealing.

One way to begin is by choosing a pair of comfortable chairs to place on either side of the fireplace. Identical chairs offer an easy solution, but you could also pick chairs with a similar style, size, and scale.

Next, place your sofa parallel to the fireplace, away from the chairs but close enough to create a cozy conversation area. Set a large coffee table or ottoman in front of the sofa. An imaginary line drawn from the center of the fireplace should bisect all these pieces.

Arrange paired accents on the mantel and carry through to the coffee table.

CENTER OF ATTENTION *top* In this typical symmetrical arrangement, seating is floated in the middle of the room. Anchor a fireside grouping with an area rug. Face the chairs and sofa toward each other to encourage conversation. Frame the space with more seating and cabinets for storage.

WARM AND WINNING *right* A perfectly balanced room can appear formal and stiff. To relax the look, interject some casual fabrics or unexpected colors and textures. In this fireplace setting, the painting's warm tones inspired the chairs' energizing hue.

CONVERSATIONAL CUES *opposite* With its symmetrical arrangement of furniture, lamps, and even groupings of wall art, this room could have felt intimidating. But turning the easy chairs toward each other (while still facing the fireplace) encourages socializing.

Symmetry

PRETTY PAIRINGS *above* The rules of symmetry are established by the matching loveseats, windows, and side chairs in this elegant parlor. Accessories break those rules without disturbing the feeling of equilibrium. On the mantel, a white hippo balances the taller but more ephemeral arrangement of feathers. And on the coffee table, a driftwood candelabra faces off with a frothy vase of flowers.

TWICE AS NICE *right* Order is assured by a centrally located fireplace and paired easy chairs and side tables. Eye-catching accents—a sunburst mirror and a tall tripod lamp with a drum shade—add just enough visual weight to keep the arrangement lively.

finesse your fireplace with built-ins

With custom cabinetry, you can enhance the status of a fireplace as a room's focal point—while adding copious storage in a small footprint.

- Make built-ins look like they belong. Your goal should be to make new cabinetry look original to the home, so start by studying the existing space. The style, materials, and colors of new cabinetry should complement existing structural features. Adding built-ins on either side of the fireplace pleases the eye by enhancing architectural symmetry.

- Know what you want to store before locking in features and sizes. Plan high shelves for displaying photos and collectibles; consider accent lighting to showcase your favorite pieces. Medium-height shelves work well for books or other objects frequently accessed. Closed cabinets hide the clutter of electronic gear, games, and even fireplace tools. Built-in benches expand seating options for special occasions; with hinged seats, they boost storage potential.

- For a finished appearance, match the size of a TV niche to the television set being installed. Leave a little extra room to ventilate heat from electronics. Add openings at the rear or side of the niche for wires, cables, and cords.

Symmetry

MIRROR IMAGE
opposite Matching large mirrors on either side of this fireplace increase the perceived size of the room.

LIBRARY LAYOUT *above*
This library's balanced layout gives each focal point its due. Matching sofas are positioned so that each offers views of the fireplace, a bookcase, and the landscape beyond tall windows.

POWER OF ART
above right
Furniture and accessories pull their colors from the eye-catching canvas above the fireplace. With the sofas and walls so similar in hue, it's the pillow colors and fireplace that enliven the room.

BIG AND BEAUTIFUL *right*
Make a monolithic fireplace inviting. Pull plush sofas close to the fire for a cozy seating group. This wide mantel holds large-scale objects that suit the room's style.

Open Rooms

A large space calls for a grand fireplace. Ensure that the model you choose creates an adequate presence to suit the scale of your room.

Buy an existing home, and you make the best of the fireplace you've inherited. Build a new home or an addition, and you can plan your fireside down to the last detail. Make it count—especially if you have an open floor plan.

You'll want to avoid lots of undefined space that feels cold and unfocused. High ceilings and an absence of walls may leave furnishings adrift. So in addition to the fireplace, take advantage of ceiling beams, a change in ceiling height, or an amazing view to define activity areas within the space. Partial walls or perimeter pillars also provide good cues. Arrange the furniture in each area so that the fireplace can be seen (if you can raise the hearth 12 to 18 inches above the floor, all the better). Make sure one area focuses on the hearth, radiating outward, with an ample area rug to anchor the grouping by creating a room-within-a-room experience.

ADJOINING SPACES *top* There is no need to crowd your furniture when you have a large open space, as seen here; leave room for traffic and an entry drop spot. Cozy key pieces up to the fireplace, facing each other and the fireplace. Use side tables to bookend the grouping.

STYLISH SEPARATION *right* Multiple furniture groupings suit a large room with multiple uses. In this light-filled space, a sofa, chair, and coffee table create an intimate conversation spot in front of the fireplace. By the window, a bookcase prompts another grouping; this time to facilitate working. Using the same golden-stained oak throughout unifies the space.

Floral-print
armchairs and a
nubby sisal rug link
this living room
to the garden, a
key part of the
room's experience.
The large mirror
expands a room
already opened
up by a wall of
windows.

Open Rooms

ACTION ZONES
Pulling furniture close to the hearth creates an intimate spot for socializing, while a rectangular table and chairs mark the dining area. A wide, clear path makes it easy to access French doors to the patio.

BEAUTY IN BALANCE *above* In this visually balanced room, an easy chair holds its own against a beige sofa because of its colorful floral upholstery. The table and antique chairs add a stately presence.

COHESIVE SPACES *right* A sofa and end table suggest a wall between a casual living room and kitchen. Warm taupe paint on the fireplace surround and kitchen cabinetry unifies the two areas.

CHANGE OF PACE *below* Anchored by the fireplace, conversation rules in this quartet of chairs—three streamlined, one ornate—circling a pedestal dining table.

SWITCH PLACES *below right* White walls and woodwork create a blank canvas in this open space. Flipping the usual order of things, a dining table hugs the hearth, and a comfy conversation grouping is stationed by the stairs.

Open Rooms

SILVER SPOTLIGHT *right* Flanked by seating areas (one embraced by a bay window), a classic fireplace topped with a mirror becomes the focal point for both. A pathway through the middle of the room makes it easy to claim a spot to relax.

FLEXIBLE FASHION *below* Mimicking the functionality of a sectional, this L-shape arrangement of furniture can be rearranged to focus on the view instead of the fireplace. A small area rug enhances the room-within-a-room perception.

LIGHTER AND BRIGHTER *opposite top* Oversize sofas and a dark fireplace surround suggest a substantial framework for arranging furniture. But a glass-top coffee table, slender side tables, and the mantel's matching glass vases lighten the visual load in this fireside scene.

JUST US TWO *opposite bottom* Matching armchairs and a rattan storage ottoman create a snug spot for visiting in front of the fire. Antique accent tables with turned legs offer striking landing pads for snacks and Chinese porcelain.

traffic flow
Plan your layout to make a room livable as well as stylish.

Surrounded by rooms, hallways, and doors, a great-room is your home's equivalent of a busy highway interchange. That's why you need to direct traffic with savvy furniture groupings. Create a circle of pieces around the hearth, marking the "no through-traffic" zone with an area rug. Honor the room's natural pathways between points, preserving conversation clusters and sight lines to the TV or a spectacular view. Replace a ponderous coffee table or bulky sofas with easy-to-move accent tables or a sleek sectional instead.

Multiple Focal Points

Your fireplace can be a team player, cheerfully sharing the spotlight with a widescreen TV or a wide-open view.

Its architectural mass alone makes the fireplace a natural focal point. Add the promise of warmth, a suggestion of romance, and the beauty of flames, and it's hard to believe anything else could grab all the attention.

Yet there are other possibilities. Whether windows reveal an exciting skyline, a body of water, or lush gardens, you'll want everyone to see it all—without giving up the benefits of a hearth. Another culprit? Televisions, sometimes reaching 60 inches or more and growing wider all the time. What's a homeowner to do?

Group two or more focal points. Instead of a mirror or painting, mount your TV above the fireplace or place it in a built-in niche to the side. Build your fireplace on an outside wall. Frame it with wide floor-to-ceiling windows to draw attention to, rather than compete with, the view.

CHANGE FOCUS *top* As seen in this example, use an L-shape sectional to focus attention on both fireplace and television. Arrange chairs so they don't obstruct traffic flow, choosing models that swivel to face the sofa, fireplace, or TV. Group tables with seating to serve as handy landing spots for drinks and snacks.

CITY VIEW *right* Although the fireplace makes a handsome focal point, it's the skyline view that stars here. The furniture grouping is widespread—facilitating traffic to doors that lead to the beach. Visually lightweight pieces—a glass-top coffee table and Louis XIV chairs—enhance the room's airy personality.

THREE AT ONCE Clustering multiple focal points—a fireplace, artwork, and an aquarium—means one furniture arrangement serves them all. Matching sofas and an easy chair face the hearth; the aquarium is large enough to accommodate viewing from multiple angles.

Multiple Focal Points

TV TERRITORY
opposite Next to the fireplace, a custom built-in creates a second focal point with a niche that puts the TV at eye-level for seated viewers. Fireside seating offers a clear view of both areas, with a coffee table stationed to hold drinks and books.

OCEAN ACCESS
top Orange leather armchairs mark the boundaries of a seating zone whose focus can instantly shift among fireplace, TV, aquarium, and ocean view. Streamlined loveseats flank the fireplace, stationed outside of the priority seating area but accessible for guests.

COOL COLLECTIONS
center A raised hearth makes it easier to see the flames in this grouping that embraces traffic. Built-in shelves put collectibles and photos on display near the windows, where eyes want to linger.

BUILT-IN BEAUTY *right* A wall of cabinetry gathers multiple focal points into an organized whole. The television's offset placement is balanced by display shelves on the opposite side.

Change focus quickly by picking pieces that are easy to move: a sectional, chairs on casters, and light tables.

Multiple Focal Points

fireplaces & TVs

Believe it: Your fireplace can coexist with a widescreen TV.

Television sets, which grow bigger with each new innovation, compete with fireplaces in any room where people gather. Your challenge is to help these amenities share the spotlight—stylishly.

Today's digital TVs offer a solution not possible for chunky analog models: that of being installed above the fireplace mantel. This space-saving application allows you to concentrate two focal points on a single wall, which means the same furniture grouping can work for both.

For a seamless look, place your TV in custom-built cabinetry that complements the fireplace—either by assimilating the mantel and surround, or by repeating key materials. The same installation can incorporate bookcases, display shelves, and enclosed cabinets for additional electronic components, games, and more.

In a long room, center the fireplace on an end wall, and place the TV set on the opposite wall. Position sofas back to back in the center of the room: one facing the hearth, the other facing the TV.

CINEMA SEATING *left* The major pieces of furniture, arranged outward from a widescreen TV above the mantel, anchor this multiuse living space. Built-in storage on the side includes drop-down linen shades to hide clutter and streamline the view on movie night.

COLORFUL CAMOUFLAGE *top* This television is cleverly disguised by sliding panels (shown open here) that look like a single piece of art. Open them to enjoy a favorite show. Close them to put the focus on fire-warmed conversation.

FRESH FOCUS *above* With walls painted a bright green, it's the room's white mantel, bookcases, and woodwork that attract attention. The TV is mounted within a frame painted the same color as the walls, causing electronics to play second fiddle to the fireplace when not being used.

Unusual Spaces

Whether you need to organize an open area or add interest to an awkwardly shaped room, start by anchoring the space with a fireplace.

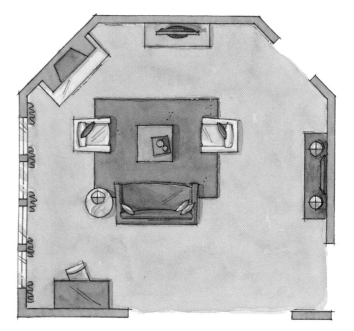

If your room has odd angles, irregular ceiling heights, or unexpected nooks, don't despair. When your room has a fireplace, even an off-center one, you get a strong visual element around which to focus furnishings and the activities that go with them. Add an area rug to further define the space and anchor the grouping.

An unconventional space may be more challenging to decorate, but it's also more visually dynamic.

CORNER VIEW
top Keep the TV and an off-center fireplace, seen in this example, near each other so that both can be viewed from every angle. Float furniture to focus on the two, with an area rug anchoring the grouping. Place a computer desk and storage console on perimeter walls.

ANGLED ATTRACTION
right An angled wall increases a fireplace's visibility. And when that wall intersects with doors that open to a pool, the fireplace gets equal billing with an irresistible amenity. Arranging the furniture in a rectangle parallel to the main wall makes the best use of floor space.

WINDOW WALL
A cozy fireside grouping of brown leather chairs balances the soaring openness of a vaulted ceiling sheathed in white. The room's panoramic view demands a flexible furniture arrangement that can regroup as needed to admire Mother Nature.

Unusual Spaces

GRAY SHADES
right With its asymmetrical placement on an angled wall, this fireplace makes room for the real star: a dramatic painting whose swirls of gray are echoed in the long sofa's velvet upholstery.

CORNER CAPTIVE *below* Although tucked in a corner, the fireplace and TV are visible throughout this multipurpose room. Flanked by glass and floating against a white background, both focal points feel right at home.

basement fireplaces
Do your homework before adding a fireplace to a lower-level room.

Want to enliven a dark and uninviting basement? Install a fireplace. But consult a pro first. Decide whether you want the fireplace for looks or to use as a heat source. Be ready to discuss the size of the space and existing structures or window openings. Solve any moisture problems and know what mechanical systems you have available before installation.

TUCKED AWAY *above* Flanked furniture groupings allow a clear view of this arched fireplace niche.

SHOW AND TELL *above right* Furniture placement maximizes the view, but the fireplace gains prestige in colder weather.

COLOR CUES *center right* Mismatched chairs echo the colors in the irregular stones making up the fireplace surround.

SINGLE MINDED *center far right* Three focal points, including an in-cabinet TV behind doors, dictate the arrangement.

MOUNTAIN VIEW *below* A cozy grouping around a massive hearth makes an intimate setting in a spacious room.

FIRESIDE CHAT *below right* This fireplace divides a larger space, making a seating group cozy and intimate.

decorate
a fireplace

One of the real pleasures—and challenges—of having a fireplace is decorating it. You may feel like a painter standing in front of a blank canvas: eager to begin, but anxious about getting it right. In this chapter, you'll learn simple strategies for decorating a mantel, using color to add personality, and keeping an unlit fireplace from feeling dreary. You'll also glean ideas for playing up a fireplace during the holidays. The end result? Helping your fireplace glow as a focal point all year long.

Clean or Busy

Are your mantel and hearth full? Or beautifully bare? Use the way you fill the space around the fireplace to reflect your personal style.

Take a look around the room where your fireplace is—or will be one day. Is the area filled with accessories or left purposely undecorated? If your matching love seats are buried under a dozen embroidered throw pillows, chances are you'll lean toward the same feeling of abundance for the fireplace. If, on the other hand, your super-slim modern sofa stands in solitary splendor, you may want to choose a single important object for your hearthscape.

You'll create the most intriguing effect by introducing a variety of shapes, heights, and textures. Gather several decorative items with a range of silhouettes: tall and slim, round, ethereal, or chunky. Arrange them in a variety of ways, changing their relationships to one another and the amount of space between them. Step back and see what you've done. Add or subtract objects until you create a look you like.

SPOTLIGHT ROOM *top* Texture rules in a fireplace that pairs a fieldstone slip with beaded-board TV doors. Instead of a crowded display, this shelf boasts a small grouping including a single fuchsia orchid in a bright blue pot.

REFLECTED BEAUTY *right* A large, tall object balances several smaller ones nestled together to boost their visual weight. Overlapping shapes creates interest, as does placing them in front of a mirror that reflects the whole room.

INITIAL OFFERING *opposite* A group of family monograms appears in a cluster balanced by pieces of art leaning against the brick chimney.

object lessons
Add personality to your display.

Select display pieces that boast great forms and hold interest on their own. Boost appeal by layering larger pieces in the background and shorter ones up front. Give small collectibles bigger impact by grouping them. Add interest by elevating same-size pieces on books or boxes.

Clean or Busy

FRAMED FOCUS
opposite This vibrant landscape offers all the accent a plain white mantel needs. On the hearth, earthy tones of beeswax candles and birch logs blend into the surround.

ASIAN INFLUENCE
top right Elaborate architectural trim makes the fireplace mantel a suitable stage for antiques. All objects, including the bronze sconces, stand in a symmetrical arrangement that suits their stature.

GALLERY STYLE
top, far right Shapely collectibles might have gotten lost against this brick surround. Instead, framed artworks stand out against a mottled background.

SERENE GREEN
center right In keeping with this room's soothing palette, simple shapes in neutral hues adorn the mantel.

TINY TIMEPIECE
center, far right Blooms create a mantel-top arbor for a miniature clock. Alone, the clock would have been missed, but perched atop a stack of books it speaks volumes.

BLUE NOTE *right* Candlestick lamps bookend matched sets of ornaments on the mantel. The blue figurines are echoed by the foo dogs on the hearth.

achieving balance
Go back to basics when it comes to choosing what's around your hearth.

Good design is based on balance: a sense that what fills up one side has the same visual weight as what fills the other.

Symmetry: This evenhanded approach to arranging objects creates a soothing impression of order and harmony. Center a painting or mirror above the mantel, then flank it with groupings of identical-size objects. Both sides of the composition will look about the same.

Asymmetry: Use elements with different shapes, sizes, and patterns. You may have three vases on one side of the mantel and a large statue on the other, for example. They're not the same, but they are visually in sync. This type of design creates a dynamic, informal composition.

Mantel Display

Make the most of your mantel's prime decorating real estate by using color, shape, height, and texture to express your personal style. Let your eye be your guide.

The mantel shelf offers a changeable decorating platform. Any object you put there can be moved or replaced on a whim, changed with the seasons, or left in place indefinitely. Here are some strategies to stir your creative potential.

Repetition on a theme: Display similar items you love, such as matte green pottery. Even with different sizes and shapes, they'll be similar enough to create a visual whole.

The upside-down T: If you've got high ceilings, hang a large element or grouping up the fireplace wall. Then place additional items along the mantel to bring the focus back down to eye level.

The one big thing: When you've got the perfect mirror or painting to display but the mantel seems bare, choose simple pieces that don't detract. No mantel? A single bold object eliminates the need to do any further decorating.

GLASS ACT
right These glass bottles may appear to be randomly grouped. But their asymmetrical arrangement appears unified through the repetition of color and material—the flowers as well as the blue glass. The translucent forms also add interest without detracting from the artwork.

COLLECTION CUE *opposite* Miniature Statues of Liberty and Eiffel Towers have been carefully placed to fit the space between mantel and artwork. Lining them up from biggest to smallest also keeps the eye moving toward the mantel's center medallion.

Mantel Display

ABSTRACT NOTION With bold shapes on a showstopping canvas, the mantel had almost reached its decorative limit. A single vase of branches and a small glass bottle add a simple splash of color.

GILT-Y PLEASURES *top left* Gilt-framed seascapes command attention above a mantel supported by decorative corbels. Overlapping helps the small painting compete with the larger landscape's more elaborate frame and vibrant colors.

EVEN HANDED *top center* Four identical white pots planted with succulents mark the center of this symmetrical mantel display. Behind them are two framed prints; they're not precisely the same, but carry the same visual weight.

COLOR CODED *above* Although different in almost every other way, the architectural salvage and decorative arts objects in this living room share similar colors that carry the eye from mantel's end to the built-in shelves and back again.

NEUTRAL ZONE *center, far left* A white statue nearly disappears against the white wall and mantel but provides a solid mass to transition from an elaborate black frame to the black sea fan.

JUST RIGHT *center left* An amber bottle calls attention to a similar splash of color within the nearby painting. The sizes of the objects—from petite ceramics to tall candlesticks—are coordinated with the painting's position so their silhouettes never interfere with brushstrokes.

BOTANICAL BEAUTY *far left* Gentle sepia tones in the framed print, taupe planters, wood candlesticks, and stacks of vintage books add interest without shouting. The only color is the green of the leaves that ties in with the botanical print.

LOVELY LAYERS *left* Graduated sizes of framed mirrors lead the way to a window seat that offers a sunny spot for reading. A bountiful yellow bouquet stands out against the black hearth, drawing attention to the glowing pear up above.

Using Color

Adding color to the fireplace wall accentuates the beauty of the surround. Feeling brave? Take the plunge and give your fireside a vibrant personality with a bold new hue.

If you've always lived with neutral surroundings, changing the fireside wall's color seems like a big decision. But in reality, a change of paint color for the walls or surround—or both—offers an easy, inexpensive, and impressive fix.

Figure out what character you want the room to have. Neutrals such as gray, brown, and champagne imply elegance. Bright blues and yellows send out cheerful vibrations. Red signals warmth and passion. Saturated colors tend to energize, while softer shades are usually restful. So to create a haven, temper your color choice by mixing in plenty of white.

Pick a color in an area rug, fabric, or work of art chosen for the room. Contrasting a bold wall color with a white mantel will spotlight the fireplace. The same color paired with a stained wood surround creates an old-world look that integrates the fireplace into the room.

RED HOT *right* It's traditional style on the wild side when the walls, woodwork, and the fireplace surround are covered with red paint. All that crimson coverage highlights the decorative accessories, especially the mirror and the library books on adjoining shelves. A glossy paint sheen ensures the crown molding and other woodworking details still get noticed.

COOL SCHOOL *opposite* Cool gray-painted walls, a white surround, and carpet create a soothing retreat. The fireplace melts into the wall, giving the eclectic lineup of accents an ethereal foundation.

Using Color

TILE STYLE Dappled with earthy colors, a tile slip stands out from pale gray woodwork in a room that combines classic architecture with midcentury-modern chairs. Aqua-blue Mason jars sparkle on the mantel.

NESTING INSTINCT *above* Jambs and lintel painted in the same green as the walls means the objects on the mantel earn extra acclaim.

PANEL PRESENTATION *top right* With an eye to mixing old-world and trendy, a traditional surround framed by a tangerine paneled wall is a surprise.

FIRESIDE FUN *right* Multicolor field tiles set the tone for a whimsical room filled with varying shades of primary hues.

DRAMATIC ARTS *below* Charcoal-gray painted walls give a white fireplace the power to mesmerize—especially when it's topped with a gold sunburst mirror.

ATTENTION GETTER *below right* A dramatic coral accent wall frames the stark white-and-black fireplace with added warmth.

Holiday Decorating

Lucky you! You've got a built-in display space in a focal-point position. So make the most of your fireplace during the holidays, even if display time is limited.

Mantels are made for holidays. During the Christmas season, they're the spot to hang stockings, of course. But mantels and hearths make wonderful places to decorate for Thanksgiving, Hanukkah, or even Halloween.

Is your traditional fireplace framed with stately architectural trim? Play up the classic details with timeless silver elements. Or maybe your country-style fireplace pairs a knotty-wood mantel with a rough-hewn stone surround. Go rustic, with a garland of pine boughs, piles of pinecones, and bright red accents to add color.

Simple vases filled with paperwhite narcissus can highlight a contemporary slate fireplace. A high ceiling may call for an enormous wreath on the fireplace wall. In the end, your holiday decorating may be temporary, but it should look like it belongs in the room year 'round.

CREATIVE LICENSE *Look closely at the images on these two pages, and you'll see that every holiday scene starts with the same fireplace. That's the beauty of a white mantel with a white wall behind it. Together they create a blank canvas upon which you can create any look you want.*

PHOTO OPP *right* From a distance, it's the fresh green wreath that earns top billing. But come closer, and you'll see glass cylinder vases displaying photos kept in place with ornaments. The symmetrical lineup includes lilies, votive candles, and a garland of green teardrop ornaments.

keeping it secure

These ideas avoid damaging walls or mantels.

Hang in there. Removable, adhesive hangers hold artwork securely and come off cleanly without surface damage.

Lean on me. Lean framed holiday artwork against the overmantel for support.

Hold it steady. Keep figurines and picture frames stable with little dabs of specially formulated wax. These products are a bit stickier than modeling clay but won't leave a stain or residue.

CITRUS NOTES *above* With a pretty print hanging above the fireplace, keep the mantel arrangement low. Trays of citrus fruits accented with pine branches move the eye across the whole display.

FESTIVAL OF LIGHTS *left* A silver menorah is the focal point in this display. A garland of blue and white Stars of David winds around the greenery, complementing the tones in the art.

CANDLE POWER *bottom left* Graduated sizes of white pillar candles allow the same artwork to shine here, while a wooden bucket filled with pine branches brings the eye back down to the hearth.

POINSETTIA PARADE *below* Festive red poinsettia foliage pops high and low. One plant has been separated into bracts that stand alone on the mantel in clear vases. The other fills the firebox void.

Holiday Decorating

SNOW JOB *left* Graceful birch trees line the fireplace wall, thanks to wallpaper with a vertical take on nature. Hand-blown glass vases hold faux snow.

CURVES AHEAD *below* Surrounded by greenery, candles and vases of ornaments radiate from a round tray in the center. Dangling below, a garland of letters spells out a classic Christmas message.

THE BUCK STOPS HERE *bottom* Greenery, pinecones, and burlap ribbon complement a show-stopping wreath embellished with pheasant feathers and a faux reindeer head.

NATURAL BEAUTY *top left* Holiday decorating can be a subtle art, as shown in this seasonal display that pairs the mantel's exuberant bundle of branches with simple white planters of emerging bulbs tucked within built-in bookcases. Splashes of red—and the occasional Santa Claus figure—help announce that Christmas is coming.

SHIMMERING SCENE *above* When an intricately framed mirror hangs above the mantel, it makes sense to focus holiday decor on objects made from silvery mercury glass. This nearly symmetrical arrangement combines highly textural glass trees with candleholders, votives, and other gleaming objects. A small wreath made from ferns adds its own holiday attitude to the mirror's surface.

LIGHT THE WAY *center* Tall candles perched in clear glass candlesticks provide twice as much twinkle when lined up in front of a large mirror. This sparkling seasonal setup also includes a pair of matching glass cylinders filled with Christmas candy, and a collection of evergreen sprigs that connects the mantelscape with the ceiling-high Christmas tree. Hanging from the top of the mirror, a small wreath adds a fragrant touch of holiday spirit.

MILKY WAY *left* This mantel display embraces the peaceful spirit of the season with softly gleaming milk-glass vessels filled with candles and fresh evergreen branches. Perched on a snow-white mantel, the vessels' translucence complements the pearly glass frame on a focal-point mirror. Surrounded by blue ornaments, a lone reindeer brings Christmas to mind in a very quiet way. Twin sconces enhance the symmetrical nature of the display, while adding an additional glow of their own.

Holiday Decorating

BLUE CHRISTMAS
Count on color to add excitement when you display aqua Christmas stockings against the red-orange bricks that line a classic fireplace. Carrying blue accents throughout the room ties the decor into a single, festive whole.

VINTAGE VALUES *right* Honor the age of your home with objects that connect the room to holidays past. This elegant surround enhances its vintage attitude with mercury-glass ornaments and Christmas trees.

HANGING AROUND *top, far right* Brightly colored Christmas stockings filled with greenery pop against the creamy tones of a stucco-covered fireplace.

WINTER WONDERLAND *center right* Silver, gold, and pale blue ornaments adorn the mantel and the Christmas tree, echoing the room's palette.

REINDEER GAMES *center, far right* A white cardboard reindeer makes a majestic focal point and surveys the room from above the mantel. Below, the firebox boasts a sparkling liner covered with gold ball ornaments.

RED, WHITE, AND BLUE *right* Decorations in reds and blues pop against sky blue walls and white furnishings. A cute firescreen adds interest down low.

CLASSIC CHRISTMAS *far right* Hand it to white mittens: They create a whimsical garland when attached to the mantel with gingham bows.

Holiday Decorating

AUTUMN HUES
Your mantel can be a Thanksgiving focal point when you display coral-color roses, autumn leaves, and mini pumpkins on a cake stand.

fright night fireplace

Hey, Christmas—don't be selfish! Let a fireplace join the Halloween fun with haunting displays.

If you only have time to decorate one spot for Halloween, let it be the fireplace. Mantels and hearths are the perfect gathering places for all your favorite Halloween accessories. Your mantel display will look smartly coordinated if you stick to a palette.

Consider this whimsical sock monkey display, *right*. Its sense of fireside fun starts with an oversize argyle pattern (a sock-monkey classic) that becomes art through the application of peel-and-stick decals. Monkeys in masquerade, garlands, and a hearth-level pumpkin parade carry out the color scheme in spirited style.

A bone-white mantel and equally ghostly walls make the perfect backdrop for a shapely collection of accessories, *below*; the clock creates a focal point around which an assortment of orange and black objects are arranged. A white pumpkin honors October 31 with its decoupaged digits.

Black and purple reign when cutout paper mansions are silhouetted against a white background, *below right*. A lone spider hangs from the edge of the mantel, while a garland of intensely purple letters screams "Trick or Treat" against the flames.

Filling the Void

Use a little creativity to keep your fireplace bright and appealing when it's too warm outside to build a fire.

Although there are few sights more welcoming than a brightly burning fire, the black hole of an unlit fireplace can be an unwelcome focal point. If you're looking for a summertime fill-in, try one of these solutions to add a stylish glow without flames.

Create the impression a fire is just moments from being built by stacking logs on the grate.

Fill the opening with a lush green plant or a basket of colorful summer annuals, which works best if the fireplace receives a fair amount of daylight.

Keep the firebox interesting by adding a decorative fire screen.

Romance a dark firebox with a display of chunky candles. Rest them on a heatproof base to catch dripping wax.

Adorn the space with weathered mementos. Shop flea markets for timeworn shutters to mask the firebox, or set out a platter of seashells or pinecones.

LOGGED ON *top* Birch logs do a great job of brightening this dark firebox because of their white bark and papery texture. Propping them up in baskets aboard pieces of stone gives the display a vertical look that fits the space. Try to find baskets that match the style; in this example, handmade baskets suit the rustic brick surround with their earthy textures.

ARTISTIC ATMOSPHERE *right* Summertime suits a room decked out in sherbet colors. All the bright pinks, yellows, oranges, and greens demand an equally lighthearted treatment on the hearth, offered here by a polka-dot screen simply propped up against the surround.

INDOOR GARDEN Bring nature indoors with a lush grouping of plants, each one thriving in its own plain white pot. This artful display succeeds because of its variety, both in the types of succulents and in the vessels used as planters.

Filling the Void

SHELL GAME
Intricate sea forms
stand out against
the dark lining
of the fireplace.
Displayed on plain
black stands, the
shells' pale colors
complement the
colors and textures
of the mosaic-tile
fireplace.

ECO FRIENDLY *above* The lush fronds of a Boston fern break out of the firebox, turning this unlit fireplace into a fresh green focal point.

PILED HIGH *top right* a diagonal pile of wood in the firebox adds another intriguing detail to a room bursting with color and pattern.

MATCHED SET *center right* Tall enough to hide the firebox, twin urns filled with blue-green grass bring that hue to the room's center.

GLOBAL VIEW *right* Globes replace logs and andirons in this humorous fireside tableau. Dabs of sticky wax keep the pretend planets in place.

NATURE PRESERVE *far right* It's Earth Day every day in a room decorated with blues, greens, and browns—especially when cut branches camouflage the fireplace. Blue- and white-glazed statuary decorates the hearth.

renovate
a fireplace

Stuck with a hopelessly inappropriate fireplace? Take heart—even a rough-hewn misfit can be tamed by clever design. Your fireplace may be classic, but it can still look tired or out of sync with the rest of your room or decorating scheme. If earlier remodeling efforts were poorly done, the most elegant fireplace can be stripped of its charm. The question becomes whether a major redo is necessary or just a bit of cosmetic sprucing up. When you're ready to rejuvenate your fireplace, you'll find inspiration in these stories of fireplaces with new spark.

Befores & Afters

A fireplace that's just all right may not be just right for you. You can bring out the best in your fireplace with an imaginative quick fix or a full-blown remake.

Though fireplaces are a much-desired amenity, few houses are sold by hearth alone. If the location is right, remember that the fireplace can be redone.

When planning an ambitious remake, research is key. Once you've settled on a style and materials, and the type of fireplace–wood-burning, gas or other–sketch your final design out in detail, on paper or with the help of a computer program.

One way to test your plan is to make a full-scale model of the design with cardboard; put it in place to see how your dream fireplace fits in the room—and it's much cheaper to revise a design in cardboard than in stone.

Take your ideas to a professional designer or architect. Have more than one mason or carpenter bid the job, and ask to see samples of their existing work. You're looking for a skilled craftsman who takes pride in attention to detail.

before

FANCY FACE
Converting a two-family home into a single-family dwelling offered a chance to put a more elegant face on the living room and its fireplace. Although the chimney and firebox remained intact, the entire face of the fireplace was replaced with a stone surround and warm ocher marble slip. New custom bookcases flank the reimagined focal point.

FEDERAL FIXUP A neglected 18th-century Federal-style home needed a lot of care and attention to bring it back to its former glory, but the woodwork was in surprisingly good shape. The fireplace casework, bookcase, and paneling were left in their existing condition, including the old finish—flaking paint and all—on the densely grained yellow pine and white oak. The restrained lines of this early American architectural style are echoed in the simple furnishings

before

Befores & Afters

before

RECLAIMED COMFORT At the end of a long, narrow family room, this fireplace was not an inviting destination. To give it family- and eco-friendly flavor, the walls were reclad in warm reclaimed timber that instantly added coziness and made the details of the fireplace casework stand out. To give the surround even more personality, the slip and hearth floor were replaced with mottled gray tiles that coordinate with tones in the timber. A pair of upholstered chairs and an activity table raise the comfort level.

Safety tips for rekindling an old flame.

Inspect. Unused fireplaces can attract wildlife. Even if a chimney cap is screened, bugs, small birds or rodents, and debris may clog the shaft. Look for possible damage from the elements. Water and ice can crack the flue or chimney.

Ask questions. If the fireplace is unused in a house you're thinking of buying, ask why. Poor draw or a flue fire mean there are repairs you'll have to make before you can use the fireplace again.

Clean and repair. Small cracks in the chimney exterior can be a careful DIY repair, but for most fireplace fixes and chimney cleaning, you should hire a professional chimney sweep.

before

UNITY RULES Winterizing a sitting room with a wall of windows meant adding a wood-burning fireplace that, in its beautiful details, mirrored the existing one in the room directly behind it. The fireplace surround features an organic scroll shape that flows alongside the ikat fabric used on the chairs that flank it and echoes the elegant curves of the table between the chairs. Besides providing an additional source of heat in the winter, the thoughtfully designed addition supplies architectural rigor and permanence year 'round.

Befores & Afters

WEEKEND WONDER A fireplace facelift doesn't have to mean a major remodel. After a new wood-burning stove insert was installed in this family room fireplace, the old surround just didn't have the design chops to carry if off. So, within the span of a weekend, the shiny glazed ceramic tile was replaced with large matte granite floor tiles from floor to mantel. The mantel got a new look as well, with an unstained oak bracketed shelf reminiscent of Arts and Crafts style.

update with paint

Sometimes a new look is only brushstrokes away.

The most inexpensive way to update a fireplace is with paint. While it can be undone, painting a fireplace (brick in particular) is a big step, so choose a color or finish that works with the design of your home or your overall decorating style to ensure it will be a look you'll love for the long haul.

A long, narrow room that lacks a lot of natural light and is dominated by a dark brick fireplace can benefit from a lighter color palette that extends to the fireplace brick and mantel, *right*. When painting brick, use a roller designed for textured surfaces to get the paint into the cracks and crevices. For especially deep cracks, a brush is best. Give a plain surround new character by adding wood appliques and corbels and painting a faux marble finish on the jambs and lintel, *below*.

One way to give an old fireplace a new look and emphasize its importance in a room is to paint it a color that sharply contrasts with the surrounding walls. In this dramatic example, *bottom right,* a formerly stained fireplace gets an arresting new look with a coat of black paint. Against the magenta walls, it's impossible to ignore. When painting over old wood, use an oil-based primer to ensure smooth and even paint coverage.

Befores & Afters

DESIGN DISCONNECT This low-slung 1960s ranch had been relatively untouched since its construction, and the homeowners wanted to keep its classic form. But the large, chunky rock fireplace, with its thick slab of wood for a mantel combined with incongruous arched bookcases, was a bit too much of a midcentury muddle. Removing the cabinets and coarse rock and covering the wall with simple horizontal boards and a timeless marble and wood surround respects the home's casual ranch style with sophisticated appeal.

before

PERIOD PERFECTION The classically traditional fireplace in the living room of this 1930s Tudor was acceptable, but the homeowners had DIY dreams of giving it more period panache. The new mantel they designed matches the home's Gothic archways, while recessed panels, an augmented overmantel, which seamlessly incorporates the TV, and elaborate crown molding add architectural detail. A new built-in cabinet on one side of the fireplace balances the door on the other side.

Befores & Afters

before

JUST ENCASE Flat and featureless was the nicest thing you could say about this dated fireplace. With nothing to recommend it, the uninspiring focal point needed a new look—and the lack of ornament or depth actually made it easier. First up, an inexpensive fix for the brass-and-glass doors, courtesy of a $5 can of spray paint (remove doors and do this outside). A new slip of mottled white mosaic tile brightens the formerly dark surround, and the entire feature gets a final finish with beautifully trimmed white wood casing.

retrofit with care

There's more than aesthetics to consider when retrofitting a fireplace.

If it ain't broke. Be wary of changes that can alter the relationship between the size of the flue opening, the smoke chamber, and the firebox.

Follow codes. Local building codes spell out rules for installing a new fireplace or renovating an old one. No matter how extensive your plans, it's important to know the safety issues covered in these codes.

Go with a pro. Changes that involve the firebox should be handled by a professional installer, who will know and follow local codes governing the required gap between the firebox and floor joists or framing.

before

INSPIRED UPDATE The original dark brick and glass-and-brass doors of this dreary family room fireplace attested to its 1980s builder-home beginnings. In a complete makeover, the brick corbels and mantel were removed. A wood frame, inspired by the room's raised wainscoting, was built around the fireplace and raised hearth and painted a crisp white. An energy-efficient gas insert replaced the wood-burning firebox, and the update was finished with a slip and hearth floor of patterned ceramic tile.

1 Fireplace, 3 Ideas

Feeling like you're stuck with a ho-hum hearth? Try one of these three easy updates—manufactured stone veneer, wood paneling, or wallpaper—to give your fireplace a hot new attitude.

BLAND BEGINNINGS
right Ceramic tiles and wood trim around an open firebox are the only design elements that set off this undistinguished hearth. But the fairly flat surface offers a world of possibilities for a DIY update.

before

You've got a lovely living room, but something seems to be missing. Let's call it personality. That's what happens when the fireplace—a room's natural focal point—offers simple functionality but not flair.

Let's start with our "before." It's not awful. It's just boring Ponder our three possibilities to see how dramatically the look of a fireplace can change a room's character with a simple makeover.

Rustic Renovation To create a rugged personality, we chose to transform that bland fireplace with natural-looking stone veneer manufactured from 80

percent recycled materials, *right.* You don't need a mason for this DIY project. That's because the pieces (which are cast from real stone) are lightweight and only ½-inch to 1⅝-inches thick. They're easy to install with premixed adhesive, a putty knife, and a hacksaw.

First we removed the tile-and-wood surround to create a smooth surface. Installing rows of stone more than halfway up the bump-out wall created visual impact. A reclaimed beam tops the stone with timeworn appeal. A flat screen lends charm to the firebox.

craggy convert

Update a dull wall with stone veneer.

Prepare surfaces. Your wall must be flat, smooth, clean, and oil-free.

Work horizontally. Smear adhesive onto backs of stones (like you're icing cupcakes, not buttering toast), photo **A**, then press firmly and evenly to the wall. Alternate piece sizes as you go to break up vertical seams, photo **B**.

Cut stones to fit. Using hacksaw or power saw with masonry blade, saw stone face first, photo **C**. Remove sawdust. Position cut edges so they can't be seen.

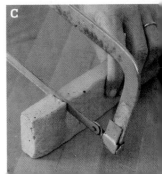

1 Fireplace, 3 Ideas

Modern Makeover Turn a less-than-winning wall into a grid made from 1×2-inch boards, *below*. For this facelift, we left the original surround in place. We divided the space into equal sections, making sure to account for the width of the wood. After cutting the trim pieces to the right lengths, we nailed them in place and caulked the edges. We took the grid all the way to the ceiling for added drama, then painted the wall and trim the same warm shade of butternut.

With the sky-high grid, there was no need for a mantel. Instead, we suspended three small wood pendants and removed the rug to add to the contemporary style.

Tranquil Transformation This stylish conversion, *opposite*, began with pale blue walls and by wrapping the bump-out with a traditional mantel created from crown molding and medium-density fiberboard supported by corbels. We painted the mantel creamy white to match the lower half of the wall surrounding the fireplace. Above the mantel, patterned wallpaper turns the formerly flat feature into an eye-catching focal point. The wallpaper's taupe tones complement the limestone-look tile below. A simple arrangement of blue glass vases and stacked books adds just the right touch of elegance.

precise planning

Make your fireplace facelift look like it was done by a pro.

One of the hallmarks of couture fashion is the exquisite care with which fabric is cut, draped, and stitched. That same attention to detail can give your remodeling efforts professional panache.

Need an example? Take the fireplace makeover at left. The repetitive squares carry your eye upward and back down again. Distort one 90-degree angle, and the resulting flaw will be obvious. The wallpapered overmantel at right carried a similar challenge. With such a large repeat, it was important to center the pattern vertically as well as horizontally. The stone-veneer fireplace on the preceding page required each row of stone to be perfectly level before proceeding to the next. So learn to love your ruler, your level, and your carpenter's square, and you'll love the results.

add a fireplace

Advances in styling and technology make it easier than ever to include a fireplace in an addition or a room remodeling project. Before you lose yourself in romantic visions of blissful evenings spent before a crackling fire, though, stop for a reality check. Think about the best type of fireplace for your needs, what your budget can afford, and what building codes and structural requirements you'll need to factor into your plan. Start by considering, the basic design components in this chapter and you'll be ready to move forward on fulfilling your dream.

Masonry Components

Available for centuries, custom-built fireplaces, also known as masonry fireplaces, can be designed to meet most any specifications.

Masonry fireplaces are a popular choice for higher-priced custom homes and historic renovations, particularly when paired with a gas starter. Wood-burning masonry fireplaces are built on site by a stonemason, making them the most expensive type of hearth to install, but they are also the most flexible in terms of a custom size and style.

The aroma of burning wood, the crackling sounds, and the glow of the fire make these hearths attractive options for a fireplace addition. Drawbacks, however, include the expense, the regular cleaning up of ashes and soot, the lingering odor of smoke, and the need to purchase and store firewood. Be aware, too, that open

A wood-burning masonry fireplace recalls the romance of a medieval castle, a mountain lodge, a cabin in the woods, or a country farmhouse.

wood-burning fireplaces, unlike sealed gas units, introduce small amounts of smoke and other emissions into a home's interior, reducing indoor air quality.

To build a basic brick masonry fireplace with a 4×3-foot opening and a 20-foot-tall chimney, plan to spend from $8,000 to $12,000. Budget additionally for the construction of a surround. The bricks, stones, and concrete required to build a custom unit will also require more structural support than a prefabricated unit, adding to the overall cost.

Know the terms

Masonry fireplaces are made up of the components shown in the illustration on the next page.

The *firebox* is the open area that contains the fire. In masonry fireplaces, this box is lined with firebrick, a type of masonry specially manufactured to withstand intense fires. In prefabricated fireplaces, the firebox is lined with metal or a refractory material that looks like masonry bricks but is lighter in weight.

The *hearth* technically refers to the floor, the part of the fireplace where the fire burns; the term is also used to refer to the entire fireplace, hence the term "hearth industry" for the fireplace business as a whole. The back hearth is the bottom of the firebox, while the front hearth extends a short distance into the room and is usually covered with a decorative and fireproof material such as brick, stone, or ceramic tile.

The *throat* is the area directly above the fireplace and below the flue. This narrow opening causes the hot air and smoke to gain speed as they enter the flue, creating a draft that keeps the fire burning properly and prevents smoke from entering the room.

The *damper* is the movable metal flap covering the throat; it is opened and closed manually. The open damper allows the fire to burn and smoke to escape. When the fire is out, the damper should be closed to prevent warm inside air from flowing up and out the chimney.

The *smoke chamber* is the space directly above the throat. This prevents downdrafts in which outside air flows down into the firebox and causes smoke to flow into the room. Smoke recirculates in this area so that ash particles are thoroughly burned before going up the chimney. The flat bottom of the smoke chamber is called the *smoke shelf.*

The *flue* is the inside of the chimney. In today's fireplaces, flues are lined with heat-resistant interlocking clay or ceramic tiles, insulated metal pipe, or cast-in-place, heat-resistant concrete. The *liner* protects the chimney walls from heat and corrosion. A cast-in-place concrete liner is effective for repairing an older chimney because it helps ensure the structural integrity of aged bricks and mortar.

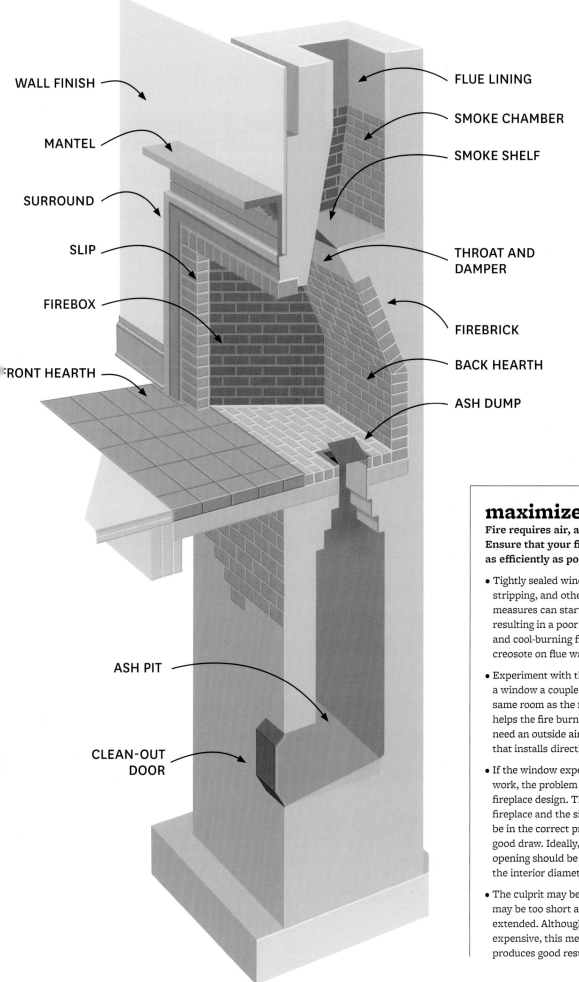

WALL FINISH

MANTEL

SURROUND

SLIP

FIREBOX

FRONT HEARTH

ASH PIT

CLEAN-OUT DOOR

FLUE LINING

SMOKE CHAMBER

SMOKE SHELF

THROAT AND DAMPER

FIREBRICK

BACK HEARTH

ASH DUMP

maximize the draw

Fire requires air, and lots of it. Ensure that your fireplace is working as efficiently as possible.

- Tightly sealed windows, weather stripping, and other energy-efficiency measures can starve a fireplace fire, resulting in a poor draw, smoky rooms, and cool-burning fires that deposit creosote on flue walls.

- Experiment with the draw by opening a window a couple of inches in the same room as the fireplace. If this helps the fire burn better, you probably need an outside air kit—a small vent that installs directly into your wall.

- If the window experiment doesn't work, the problem may lie in the fireplace design. The opening of the fireplace and the size of the flue must be in the correct proportion to create good draw. Ideally, the area of the opening should be 12 times larger than the interior diameter of the flue.

- The culprit may be your chimney: It may be too short and need to be extended. Although such work is expensive, this method usually produces good results.

Masonry Types

Know your options for masonry fireplace construction and how they can affect your enjoyment of your new hearth.

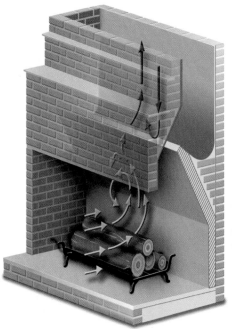

CHIMNEY CAP

There are three basic configurations of wood-burning masonry fireplaces that are still being built today.

The **Rumford fireplace** is the forebear of the modern fireplace. It is named for Count Rumford, a Massachusetts-born scientist whose 18th-century work was primarily concerned with the nature of heat. Rumford fireplaces have shallower fireboxes—just 18 to 20 inches deep—rounded throats, sidewalls angled at 45 degrees, and upright, vertical backs. The shallow firebox and angled sidewalls are designed to radiate more heat outward into the room, while the straight back allows smoke and gases to exit directly into the flue.

The **Orton fireplace** is named after Vrest Orton, author of the 1969 book *The Forgotten Art of Building Good Fireplaces*. Orton's design pitched the back wall of the firebox forward slightly to better reflect heat toward living spaces. Because the slanted back would sometimes allow smoke to drift into interiors, Orton compensated by creating a straight throat that ensured a powerful draw and eliminated smoke infiltration.

The **modern fireplace** features a steeply pitched back wall and a throat positioned well forward of the flue. This design forces smoke and hot gases to rotate just before entering the flue, ensuring complete combustion inside the firebox. Generally, this design does not radiate heat as effectively as the Rumford or Orton designs.

Cap it off

A **chimney cap** (above) is installed at the top of the stack. It keeps rain from entering the chimney, where it could mix with soot to create acidic compounds that corrode the flue lining. A cap also helps prevent drafts in particularly windy conditions. A cap should sit at least 12 inches above the end of the chimney opening.

RUMFORD

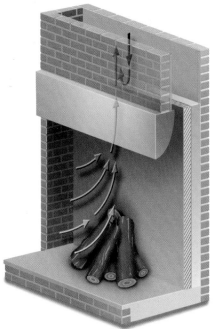

ORTON

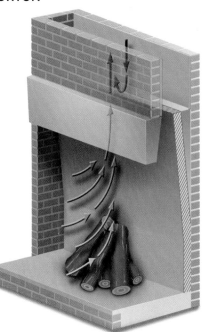

MODERN

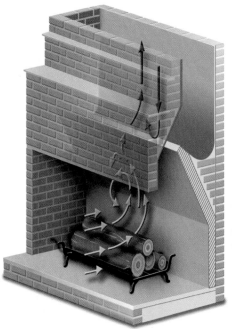

fireplace fuels

Know your woods or opt for one of these alternatives.

Wood The type of wood you use in a wood-burning fireplace, *right,* has a direct effect on both the type of fire you get and the cost of fueling your fireplace. Hard or dense woods produce an intense heat, burn longer, and produce less ash. Because of their efficiency and because they are used extensively in the building industry, these woods are also the most expensive per cord (128 cubic feet of neatly stacked wood 4 feet high by 4 feet wide by 8 feet long). Medium-density woods strike a balance between heating efficiency and cost, and are a good choice for fireplaces. Low-density woods start readily and burn fast, but they burn at lower temperatures than dense woods—a factor that allows creosote to build up on flue walls. Always use wood that is seasoned (see page 187). Purchase fresh-cut wood in the spring for use in the fall so that it dries out completely.

Gas A gas-burning fireplace, *top, far right,* burns cleaner and more efficiently than its wood-burning counterpart. Using natural gas (or propane in rural areas), the fireplace offers the convenience of turning on and off with the flip of a switch or push of a remote button.

Electric Electric fireplaces, *bottom right* run on standard household current and are ideal for DIY or retrofit situations or use in apartments, condominiums, or other locations where wood- or gas-burning fireplaces are prohibited.

Coal Anthracite coal is normally used in a freestanding stove designed to burn coal exclusively or made to burn either wood or coal.

Pellet Pellet fuel is made from recycled sawdust compressed under great pressure to form hard marble-size nuggets. Use only in stoves or inserts made for burning pellet fuel.

Gel For a low-maintenance occasional evening fire, a gel-fuel fireplace, *bottom, far right,* is an option. These fireplaces are fueled by cans of alcohol-based gel. Exercise caution when using this fuel, and never add gel fuel to a can that is already burning.

Surrounds

The frame around your fireplace is what gives it its character. Express yourself with the design and material you choose for this important component of fireside style.

Brick offers a range of traditional looks, depending on the type of brick and the installation pattern. Ceramic tile comes in a wide array of colors, patterns, textures, and sizes for the ultimate in design flexibility. Slabs, blocks, or tiles of stone—granite, marble, soapstone, slate, limestone—as well as manufactured veneers offer timeless style. Choose a polished or honed finish for a contemporary look, or rocks left in their natural state for a rustic one. Concrete surrounds can be customized to suit your design objectives. Wet concrete can be dyed almost any color and embellished by stamping or embedding objects in it before it is fully cured. Metal surrounds can be made from bronze, copper, iron, nickel, or steel in a contemporary, rustic, or vintage style depending on the finish and format. Stucco offers an old-world look that can be customized with paint.

CROWN JEWEL *right* A wall of cabinetry and architectural trim provides the framework that makes this fireplace the center of attention. The wall of wood is not fireproof, so a slip of marble protects the woodwork from flames and embers. A TV takes the place of artwork above the mantel.

SET IN STONE *opposite* As carefully shaped and pieced as a vintage picture frame, this limestone surround frames the firebox with subtle hues. Within the black metal firebox, an arrangement of birch logs complements the surround's neutral good looks.

Surrounds

LITHIC LOOKS
opposite Designed as a single dramatic entity, this contemporary fireplace surround and hearth are built from slabs of figured black marble. The stone's honed finish lets the gleaming metallic-gold vase make a showstopping artistic statement.

TILE STYLE *above* This charming surround features blue-and-white tiles that complement a collection of Chinese porcelain.

COPPER CHIC
top right Installed within a frame of ocean-hue tiles, this sleek flame-finished copper fireplace surround adds visual warmth to a sometimes chilly open-air location.

RUSTIC BEAUTY
right Rough-hewn stone forms the surround and overmantel of this rustic fireplace lined with brick. The keystone arch opening adds a graceful note.

Mantel Design

The mantel puts the final flourish over your firebox. Choose a style and material that complement the surround and other features close at hand.

A mantel doesn't have to be fireproof, which allows you flexibility in choosing materials. Consider these options.

Wood is attractive, versatile, and easy to install. New mantels can resemble old with elaborate carvings and furniture detailing, or left purposely plain to complement a contemporary or rustic motif. Carved stone mantels are elegant and timeless. They are typically made of hand- or machine-carved marble, limestone, granite, or slate. Cast-stone replicates the look but at a lower cost. Concrete can simulate the look of carved or cast stone, but is lighter weight because when used this way the material is reinforced with fiberglass. Custom looks can be achieved with different color and texture finishes. Similarly, either plaster or gypsum can be poured into molds to create intricately detailed mantels. Metal mantels can be made from aluminum, bronze, copper, nickel, iron, or steel in a variety of finishes ranging from a hand-forged look to hand-rubbed gold.

LUXURY LINES *top* Whether antique or reproduction, an elaborately carved marble mantel adds elegant vintage character to a room, especially when paired with a similarly shaped metal fireplace screen. This mantel's curvaceous silhouette continues down the frame of the firebox to the floor with a pair of shapely corbels.

RUGGED APPEAL *right* A single rough-hewn beam makes a strong statement when installed as the mantel of a traditional brick-lined firebox. The handsome beam provides a sturdy gallery for equally rustic decor.

REPEAT MOTIF
This mantel is supported by five matching brackets that boast shapely scrolled silhouettes and, like all the elaborately trimmed woodwork in the room, a satiny smooth white-painted surface.

Mantel Design

CURVE AHEAD
opposite Above a rustic stone surround, this white-painted mantel is crafted from a single beam and a row of simple curved brackets.

MIXED MEDIA
top With their heirloom detailing, a stained wood mantel and white-painted pilasters add an eclectic note to a surround built from modern oversize slate tiles.

CROWNING TOUCH *center right* A traditional wood mantel adds architectural complexity to a surround crafted from blocks of limestone.

BRANCH OUT
center, far right Made up of river rock, this imposing fireplace surround benefits from the organic whimsy of a log mantel.

MIRROR IMAGE
right Mimicking the top of an antique sideboard, this mantel combines white-painted wood with a beveled-glass mirror. Chunky scrolled corbels help the mantel compete visually with the multicolor tile surround below.

LUSH LAYERS *far right* Like frosting on a wedding cake, this white-painted mantel combines layers of architectural trim—even on the pilasters—to give the fireplace focal-point status.

Lighting

Don't take your fireplace's beauty for granted. Use interior accent lights, ceiling fixtures, and other light sources to make sure people notice its best features after the sun has gone down.

Use light to enliven your fireplace and it will stay stylishly aglow without any flames. To light a picture over the mantel, use a recessed, adjustable "eyeball" fixture in the ceiling, about 3 feet out from the fireplace wall. For a sloped ceiling, use a monopoint, surface-mount track light. To highlight the fireplace itself, use a grazing light that plays up the texture of the stone, brick, stucco, or tile. Install a recessed downlight or surface-mounted accent light on the ceiling about 18 inches from the fireplace wall. Installing a pair of wall sconces? Locate them no more than 6 inches in from the outer edges of the mantel and at least 12 inches up from the mantel shelf. Whichever light source you use, consider adding a dimmer to electrified lights for a way to change the room's mood at the touch of a finger.

TWIN TASKS
right **Perfect for traditional decor, a pair of matching candlestick lamps illuminate the mantel's elaborate carved and applied details, while making the small furniture grouping a friendlier, cozy, and more intimate spot for fireside conversation.**

TEAM PLAYERS
opposite **Multiple light sources work together to showcase this stunning fireplace. Glass hurricanes use candlelight to emphasize the artwork. A century-old chandelier lights the mantel's details. A table lamp calls attention to the room's wainscoting.**

Lighting

Turn your easy-to-forget fireplace mantel into a wow-worthy feature by adding the right light fixtures.

HIGH LIGHTS *above* A roaring fire can illuminate the hearth, but it takes recessed lights to showcase the mantel and elegant cabinetry that frame this TV-topped fireplace surround. Additional recessed lights provide task lighting near the bay window for anyone wishing to curl up with a good book.

SIDE EFFECT *opposite* During daylight hours, this fireplace's craggy stone surround is highlighted by sunlight coming in through spacious picture windows. But at night or on cloudy days, the fireplace as well as the reading corner to its left benefit from manmade lighting: a sconce above the mantel and a floor lamp by the easy chair.

alternatives
and extras

Beyond the conventional wood-burning masonry fireplace lies a world of alternatives, so choosing the right kind of fireplace for your project can be a complex decision. You'll need to determine what type of installation will best match your needs and your budget, as well as the type of fuel you'll want to burn. Some types of fireplaces are restricted regionally by building codes and state laws, so you should be aware of what is and isn't available in your area. Peruse this chapter to explore the intriguing alternatives to a traditional hearth, from wood-burning stoves to do-it-yourself faux fireplaces.

Stoves

Today's stoves go way beyond the sooty potbellied variety of Western lore to offer sleek styling and fuel efficiency.

If heating efficiency is important to you, consider a freestanding stove. Advanced combustion technology on wood-burning models reduces emissions while increasing the amount of heat transferred to your home. Efficient combustion burns up pollutants that once would have entered the atmosphere.

Be sure to select a stove designed for your particular room size. Choosing too large or too small a stove reduces energy efficiency and can cause unnecessary condensation. Look for stoves made of plate steel or cast iron at least ¼-inch thick. Better models have a "window wash" feature that blows air across the inside of the glass to keep it free of soot.

Stoves are also manufactured in gas- and oil-burning models. Like their wood-burning counterparts, these stoves tend to be highly efficient and clean-burning.

HEARTH HIGHLIGHT *top* A tiled hearth and wall behind this cast iron stove set off both the appliance and its tall chimney. With an 80-percent-efficiency rating, the simple design blends the charm of yesteryear with the technology of today.

HEAVY DUTY *right* This freestanding soapstone-clad wood-burning stove is an ideal focal point and room divider; see-through doors enable you to see the fire from both sides, and a wraparound raised hearth offers seating options and space for wood storage. This type of stove is very heavy and may require you to reinforce the floor joists.

COLOR DIVIDE
A bright red wall
ensures that this
cast iron stove
shares the spotlight
with a vivid
bookcase and blends
the vintage styling
of the stove with the
case's modern vibe.

Stoves

BETTER TOGETHER *above*
A new cast iron stove fits within an old wood-burning hearth, taking advantage of an existing chimney. Retaining the look of the original fireplace embraces the beauty of the old while adding the efficiency of the new.

STOW AND GLOW *right* This small wood-burning unit provides a convenient spot for fuel storage beneath the firebox.

MODERN METAL *opposite, top left* Sleek lines and an unobtrusive installation make this modern-style steel gas stove an ideal choice for a contemporary interior.

COZY CORNER *opposite, bottom left* This pellet stove can burn wood pellets, corn, wheat, or barley at maximum efficiencies for very cost-effective home heating while meeting strict clean-air standards.

chimney basics
Make sure your chimney size and structure matches your appliance.

All wood-burning fireplaces and stoves, as well as many gas units, require a chimney. The chimney is the escape route for byproducts of fire: carbon dioxide, smoke, water vapor, and in some cases carbon monoxide and nitrous oxide.

Not just any chimney will do for every fireplace or stove. All chimneys should be lined (chimneys more than 50 years old might not be) and sized in diameter and length for the type and dimensions of fireplace or stove in the house and for the distance to the outside. This information is provided with new, prefabricated units, and a dealer can get the information for you if you're changing an existing unit. A liner of the wrong size or material can allow the airborne soot, ash particles, and fumes to cool before they reach the chimney cap, causing them to fall back into the firebox and vent into your home, creating a potential health hazard.

Here's a rundown on the basics:

A wood-burning stove or fireplace vents directly through the roof, *top right*, or along the outside of the house, *center right*, with a flue pipe that extends above the roofline. Wood-burning stoves, inserts, and prefab fireplaces burn at high temperatures, around 1,700 degrees Fahrenheit, and require vertical flues able to withstand intense heat. A key word here is vertical; the chimney of any wood-burning appliance should exit through the roof in as straight a line as possible with few or no angles.

A direct-vent, gas-burning stove or fireplace, *bottom right*, vents directly through the exterior wall, making for an easier, less expensive installation. But natural gas fireplaces and stoves generate a lot of water vapor. Keeping condensation to a minimum is key, and a flue lining of stainless steel or aluminum is necessary. If you plan to change the fuel source or the size or type of firebox, such as converting from wood to gas, hire a professional to evaluate whether the chimney is in good shape, and to ensure that the flue liner is the right size, material, and configuration for the new unit.

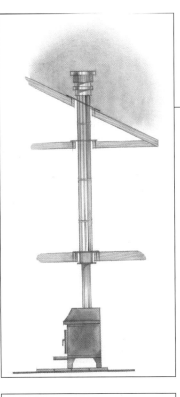

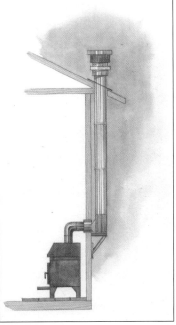

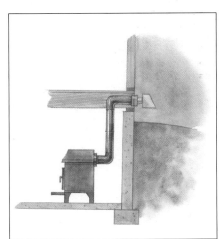

Inserts

Affordable quick-change artists, inserts upgrade old fireplaces with a minimum of fuss and mess. Available in a wide array of styles and types, you're sure to find one that suits your fancy.

Designed to fit completely inside an existing masonry fireplace or to protrude slightly, a wood-burning insert allows more heat to radiate into the room without giving up the look, sound, and fragrance of a natural wood fire.

Gas-burning inserts offer the convenience of turning on and off with the push of a remote button. There are two basic types available.

Direct-vent fireplaces use external air for combustion and expel 100 percent of the exhaust back outdoors. These units are extremely efficient and do not affect indoor air quality. Depending on the situation, pipes from the unit may run through an existing chimney flue or through an exterior wall.

B-vent fireplaces, unlike direct-vent, are not sealed from the room. Gas flames can be accessed through movable glass doors or a metal mesh curtain.

WIDE OPEN
right **The breadth of this fireplace emphasizes the horizontal wall treatment. A wide-angle view of a dramatic flame is perfect for contemporary homes and open living spaces. Inner reflective panels amplify the appearance of the stunning fire.**

TWO FACED
opposite **Create fire views in two separate rooms or feature a stunning focal point in rooms with limited space with this see-through gas fireplace. The dual-sided unit offers a cost-effective way to divide a space while maintaining an open feel.**

Inserts

GEOMETRY CLASS *above* The eye-level placement of this gas fireplace makes it possible to enjoy the cozy flames while reading in a chair, dressing for the day, or lounging on the bed. Geometric tile forms a unique surround that makes a grander statement than the fireplace would have alone.

FLUSH FINISH *right* The flush-fit design of this gas fireplace allows the slip or surround materials to be installed right to the edges of the firebox. A clean-face fireplace immediately draws the viewer's eye to the flames, creating a stunning focal point.

SLEEK AND SIMPLE *right* A low-profile facade distinguishes this direct-vent gas insert and adds contemporary flair to a rustic stone surround and raised hearth. Heavy-duty non-reflective ceramic safety glass ensures that the flames take center stage from any viewing angle.

be direct

With a direct-vent insert, a chimney is a choice.

Up and out. Direct vents exhaust gases to the outside via a single vent through a vertical pipe to the roof or by way of a short horizontal pipe that exits through an exterior wall.

Closed circuit. The same vent that releases exhaust may contain an inner sleeve that draws in fresh air to be used for combustion. These types of gas-fired units don't require indoor air for burning and are highly energy efficient.

Feel the heat. Blowers push convected heat through vents into the room while warmth also radiates through the glass doors.

Flex time. Direct-vent units can be fitted with traditional masonry or wood surrounds and vented glass doors.

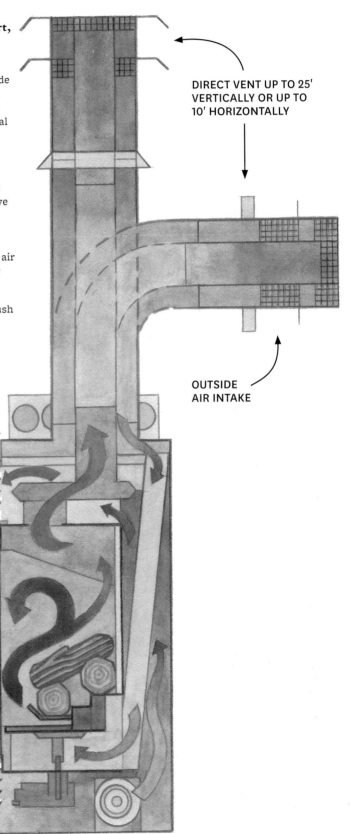

DIRECT VENT UP TO 25' VERTICALLY OR UP TO 10' HORIZONTALLY

OUTSIDE AIR INTAKE

CONVECTED HEAT

RADIANT HEAT

INSIDE AIR INTAKE

Faux

Longing for a fireplace but not quite ready to invest in a working model? Find fulfillment with a fool-the-eye version that adds visual warmth.

Every room needs a focal point, and a fireplace—real or faux—fills that bill. You can create the look of a fireplace with relative ease by installing a realistic-looking surround, then filling the unvented firebox with props. To maintain the illusion of a working fireplace, stack a narrow grate with logs, making it appear as though you were just about to light a fire. Looking to simply fill the void? Decorate the firebox with a display of pillar candles on a fireproof surface.

You can purchase vintage surrounds at flea markets, antiques shops, and architectural salvage warehouses. Choose a model that fits your space and nail it in place. Or, check home centers for kits. These projects come in a limited number of styles and sizes, but the ready-cut pieces and assembly instructions make them a convenient shortcut. For a more flexible approach, construct your own design from wood planks and molding.

TWICE AS NICE *top* Get double the functionality out of a faux fireplace by using the firebox niche for storage and display. This fireplace was created with a white-painted wood surround and tile slip and a firebox filled with wood shelves. The niche's back wall was covered with wallpaper for a splash of color.

DARK AND HANDSOME *right* In this high-contrast room, the black-painted mantel frames a firebox completely filled in with bricks. The dark red bricks create a warm backdrop for a concrete bust, while the mantel itself pops against gray walls—creating a strong center of interest around which the furniture radiates.

A new fool-the-eye fireplace complements the Victorian elegance of this room. Matching trim on the casework blends the new surround with the walls, while birch logs add to the illusion that the fireplace is original.

Faux

FRESH-AIR FLOURISH *right* A salvaged stone fireplace surround creates a pretty spot for parading plants. A single section of white wrought-iron lawn edging (a botanical equivalent to andirons) controls the greenery while complementing an equally ornate table and chairs. Puddled drapes create a temporary outdoor wall.

HEIRLOOM ATTITUDE *below* Installing an ornate crystal pendant light and antique wood surround gives a new room the look of age. In this reincarnation, the space inside the surround is filled with a patterned panel to simulate a firebox and fronted with a real screen to enhance the illusion of a working fireplace.

COTTAGE CHARM *far right* This room goes from blank canvas to cozy gathering space thanks to a mantel made from new molding and salvaged corbels with stylized floral cutouts. Flanked by bookshelves, the lap siding-lined firebox houses a gel-fuel fireplace (see page 172) that looks like a miniature cast-iron stove. An antique footrest can be pulled out in a flash for serious relaxing.

make a fake
Simple materials become a surround.

Using a pencil, mark the locations for two vertical wood boards. Using a level to make sure they're straight, secure the boards to the wall with 3-inch flathead screws or hollow-wall anchors.

Attach a horizontal board above the vertical pieces in the same way. Secure decorative brackets to the ends of the horizontal board and top with a slim shelf. Add decorative molding to your faux surround with glue.

Caulk screw holes and cracks. Prime and paint the wood. Paint the wall inside the "firebox" a dark color to add depth.

Other Options

If you don't want a traditional fireplace in your room, there are plenty of fire-breathing options: from two-sided fireplaces to ventless models that can go where they're needed.

What do you need a fireplace to do? The answer to that question will guide your research and your ultimate choice.

If you're in a condo or apartment with restrictions against wood- or gas-burning appliances, look into fireplaces powered by electricity or solid gel fuel. Both options provide realistic flames without smoke and fumes.

If you're going for drama, consider a tabletop fireplace or a wall insert—both of which offer the magnetism of fire in an unexpected location. More about the look than the heat, such models rely on glass walls for safe enjoyment of the flames.

If outdoor entertaining rocks your world, consider blurring the boundaries with a double-sided direct-vent fireplace added to an exterior wall. The see-through feature lets everyone enjoy the gas-powered flames, whether sitting inside or outside the home.

GRACIOUS DIVIDE *right* Built into a structural wall, this two-sided gas fireplace furthers the sense of flow between the living room and dining room. By raising the hearth in the lower living rom, each room benefits from the warmth and presence of a fireside focal-point.

SWEET RETREAT *opposite* Add a little heat to two rooms with a single two-sided gas fireplace, an upgrade that suits a luxurious master suite. Raising the hearth to eye level makes it easier to enjoy the flames from the bed or the vanity area next door. Tempered glass screens keep everyone safe.

Other Options

A ventless fireplace powered by electricity, solid gel fuel, or bioethanol fuel provides Fuss- and fume-free flames.

EASY BREEZY
above left Ventless electric fireplaces let you enjoy a fire without the hassle of burning wood. Many models use energy-efficient LEDs and an ember effect for lifelike flames and heat. Corner units make it easy to find a setting—no venting needed. Just plug into an outlet.

NO SMOKING
top right Small enough to fit almost anywhere, a wall-mount gel fuel fireplace can deliver flames for hours on a single burn. Gel fuel crackles like a real fire, but without odor or smoke. Backed with fiberglass insulation, this fireplace hangs on the wall.

HOT SPOT
above right Go for cozy with a fireplace table powered by gas, such as this unit, or by ethanol gel fuel or biofuel. Real flames confined by clear glass walls produce warmth and ambiance but not smoke, odor, toxic fumes, or soot.

MEDIA MAGIC
left Double your entertainment value in the same square footage by choosing a ventless fireplace combined with a home theater media center. This version includes a firebox, mantel, and shelves for media equipment, books, and DVDs.

ventless fireplaces
Get the facts on a fast-growing trend in home decor.

Before you add a ventless fireplace, consider these facts, in addition to your state's installation regulations.

Ventless gas fireplaces require gas or propane to fuel the flames. A flameproof firebox houses artificial logs that add to the illusion of a wood burn. But there are safety concerns. Carbon monoxide and other fumes can create a health hazard if the fireplace malfunctions. That's why these models include an automatic shut-off, and you may want to install a separate carbon monoxide detector. Such fireplaces also expel water vapor that can cause mold, but you can help control moisture with a portable dehumidifier.

Ventless gel-fuel fireplaces offer the look—and sound—of a real, albeit small, fire. In most cases, what you're buying is a set that includes a steel firebox, cast-concrete log set, and surround. Gel fuel is sold separately. Use this fireplace with extreme caution; never throw water on the fire, and always allow gel fuel to cool at least 20 minutes before re-lighting.

fireplace facelift
Work with the pros to get a brand new look for a dated hearth.

A fireplace lacking efficiency and good looks is a sad situation in a focal-point spot. While the temptation may be to remove everything and start over, a stylish and far less disruptive solution was the answer for this dated and drafty hearth, *top right*.

Refacing the brick surround and raised hearth was a simple fix thanks to a granite overlay fabricated to fit precisely over the existing brick. Made from a blend of 95 percent crushed granite and 5 percent polymers, the ¼-inch-thick veneer is the same non-porous and stain-resistant product used to reface kitchen countertops.

The first step is an in-home consultation to determine whether the surface is appropriate for the overlay and to choose from the large selection of colors. Then, a template is made to make an exact fit, *top, far right*. Within a couple of weeks, the two pieces for the surround and the raised hearth are ready. Professional installers adjust the pieces onsite for a snug fit and polished look, and, when ready to install, cover the back side with a layer of adhesive, *second row*. The pieces are applied to the brick surface for a perfect alignment around corners and opening, then polished with ammonia-free glass cleaner, *third row*. Finally, caulking is applied to all the joints *bottom right*. The caulk will dry to an invisible finish.

With the surface ready, a new direct-vent gas insert, *bottom far right,* completes the look. The old fireplace elements are removed, new pipes installed through the old flue, and an electrical line added for the remote start and thermostat feature. The unit is hooked up to the existing gas line, the brick firebox veneer and ceramic fiber logs installed, and the flames tested. With the hard work done, a black metal faux slip and door frame with non-reflective glass is placed over the opening and a gorgeous new single door attached, *opposite.*

Added together, the work for the entire makeover was finished within eight hours, resulting in a complete transformation that is both energy-efficient and a definite style upgrade.

Storage & Accessories

Extend your fireplace's fashion influence with stylish accessories and a convenient place to store enough firewood for immediate use.

You've got the fireplace; now you want to complement it with accessories and a wood-storage system. Unlike jewelry, which rarely has a practical use, fireplace accessories are meant to serve a purpose. Fireplace tools help you manipulate the wood and clean up embers. Andirons and grates keep logs lifted off the floor to allow air circulation, which creates a better burn. Fireplace screens prevent sparks and embers from damaging flooring and furniture. A sling made of sturdy canvas or polyester duck can be used to carry wood from outdoors.

You'll also want to store wood near the firebox. Choose from a variety of racks, usually made from sturdy metal; some have built-in hooks to keep fireplace tools handy. Or, repurpose an object big enough to hold wood for an evening's fire. If you're planning a new fireplace, consider including a niche for wood within or next to the surround.

FASHIONABLE FIRE *top* **As pretty as it is practical, this ornate metal fireplace screen is simpler than it looks; it's just a single-piece unit supported by legs. Decorative scrollwork complements the focal-point mirror and makes the screen an attractive accessory even when the fire is out.**

DOUBLE-DUTY STORAGE *right* **These built-in shelves conveniently include a box for stacked firewood and a set of fireplace tools stored in a reproduction ash bucket. Most fireplace tool sets include a long-handled brush and shovel for cleaning ashes from the hearth, and a poker for rearranging burning wood.**

GRATE WORK
Fireplace grates
serve the same
function as andirons:
supporting firewood.
Keeping the wood
off of the hearth
floor lets air
circulate, creating a
more efficient burn.

DAD

Storage & Accessories

WOOD BLOCKS *opposite* Nifty niches hold a week's worth of firewood in this brick fireplace wall. The built-in openings create visual balance for the decorative owl andirons in the firebox and the antique tortoise shell hanging above.

ACCENT ON STORAGE *above* Add a sturdy, stylish storage component to your hearth with a log rack that holds fireplace tools as well as fuel. Heavy-duty steel construction means the unit won't tip over or crumple under the weight of wood. Three attached hooks hold a poker, brush, and shovel.

RUSTIC PURPOSE *top right* Be creative with your fireplace accessories. A rustic stone fireplace calls for a repurposed crock to hold kindling or seasoned wood. The 10-gallon size shown here can hold enough logs for an evening's fire. Choose a crock with handles to make it easier to transport when fully loaded.

ARCH LOOK *right* Space-smart accessories, such as this arch design fireplace screen, also include storage options for fireplace tools. This hinged screen includes built-in hooks on the side panels that hold the included poker, shovel, broom, and tongs at the ready.

SCREEN GEM *far right* Keep it simple but elegant with a single-panel fireplace screen in a classic style. These types of screens fit most fireplace openings; their job is to look good while framing the flames and keeping sparks from escaping your fireplace.

fireplace
maintenance

Whether you do the work yourself or employ professionals, proper installation and periodic maintenance ensure that your fireplace will run safely and efficiently for decades. In this chapter, you'll find advice on building a fire that burns cleanly, safety measures every homeowner should take, and the basics of cleaning the hearth and chimney. A glossary will help you understand industry and architectural terms, and a resource guide provides a listing of fireplace manufacturers, sources for unique surrounds, and industry organizations.

Maintenance & Safety

Use your fireplace properly to ensure that your hearth adds pleasure and ambiance, not headaches, to your home life.

Fireplace chimneys and fireboxes should be checked annually to ensure the system is working properly, to prevent any problems, and, in the case of gas units, to replace materials such as faux embers. Glass doors should be checked for cracks—do not use the fireplace until any cracked glass is replaced—and cleaned with a non-abrasive ammonia-free household window cleaner. Clean only when the unit is completely cooled.

Hazards such as chimney fires can be avoided with an annual inspection, conscientious fireplace upkeep, and an understanding of the best ways to build and maintain fires in the hearth.

Weather will take its toll on your chimney. Carefully examine the masonry on the interior and exterior of your chimney. If it is cracked or damaged, it must be repaired or replaced.

Burning wood

One of the best ways to keep a wood-burning fireplace operating at peak efficiency and safety is to build and maintain proper fires. Properly constructed fires burn cleanly and are less likely to produce creosote, a flammable tarlike substance that can build up inside flue walls and ignite into a roaring chimney fire. Properly tended fires provide more heat, produce less creosote, and leave fewer ashes, reducing cleanup chores.

Before you put match to kindling, make sure the damper is open and the firebox is free of old ashes. Leftover ashes may impede airflow and reduce a fire's ability to burn efficiently. With the grate centered in the firebox, crumple two or three sheets of newspaper and stuff them under the grate. Place pencil-diameter kindling above the paper, on top of the grate. Crisscross the kindling to create air spaces all around the fuel—packed kindling will not burn properly. Over the kindling, place 1- to 2-inch-diameter pieces of wood, again in a crisscross pattern. Don't add large pieces yet.

With the damper open, place your hand near the throat of the flue and check for air movement. Downward movement or no movement at all usually means the flue is cold and needs to be warmed. To heat the flue, twist two or three sheets of newspaper into a cone. Using the narrow end as a handle, light the larger end and hold it near the throat of the flue. The resulting updraft should pull smoke and flame up the flue. Be careful handling the lit newspaper. When the cone has

burned halfway down, use it to ignite the newspapers under the grate. Once all the wood has started to burn with a vigorous flame, add large pieces in a crisscross pattern to facilitate airflow.

Once the fire is going well, add cordwood, two or three pieces at a time. Keep the fire burning vigorously. If the fire is allowed to die down and smolder for long periods, it may burn at temperatures cool enough to allow creosote to form on the flue walls. When you are nearly finished with the burn, allow the fire to die out naturally. Never pour water on a fire to extinguish it—the extreme change in temperature may crack the firebox. Don't close the damper until the fire is completely out.

Fireplace candles

If you long for the flicker of real flames in a faux or inoperable fireplace, you can add a warm glow with a display of stout candles. Look for wrought iron, pewter, or other metal candle racks or candle "trees." These multi-arm stands hold 6 to 12 pillar candles in staggered rows. You can also create your own display. Avoid placing candles directly on the hearth. Instead, rest each on a heatproof base of metal, glass, or brick to catch the drippings. Follow these tips to keep your display of glowing candles safe:

- Limit the number of candles. Too many candles can overheat the firebox.
- If your fireplace is operable, open the flue and the glass doors. Otherwise, move the candles to the front of the firebox.

- For safety, place a decorative metal firescreen in front of the candles.
- Be sure the room is adequately ventilated; burning candles use a surprisingly large amount of oxygen.
- Have a fire extinguisher available and never leave burning candles unattended.

Safety first

Building a fire inside your home requires common sense about safety.

Always keep a fire extinguisher handy for putting out small fires caused by errant sparks. Install a Class ABC fire extinguisher near the fireplace, and make sure every member of your household knows where it is and how to use it. Most fireplace stores have small, decorative fire extinguisher storage units that can be installed in easy-to-reach locations near the fireplace. Check the indicator on the extinguisher monthly to make sure the unit is fully charged. Never underestimate the hazard of an uncontained fire, no matter how small. Finally, recognize that fighting a fire is secondary to alerting everyone inside the house to evacuate and calling the fire department.

Install and maintain smoke detectors according to the manufacturer's instructions. Your home should have one in each main living area, in each hallway, and inside each bedroom. Test the detectors periodically and change batteries in battery-backup units and battery-operated units annually.

Burn only firewood or firelogs in your fireplace—never things such as pine boughs, books, gift wrap, or scrap lumber. In addition to creating harmful gases, these materials can float out of your chimney and cause a roof fire on your home or a neighboring house.

In a wood-burning unit, use seasoned wood. When wood is not properly seasoned, it has a tendency to pop and spark more, increasing the risk of flying sparks and embers. If this happens, do not add any more wood to the fire, and protect the area in front of the fire with a fireplace screen or by closing the glass doors. Note that not all glass doors can withstand the heat of a fully burning fire, so consult your owner's manual before shutting the doors.

Never leave a fire unattended. If you must leave your house before a wood-burning fire burns completely out, smother flames with baking soda, sand, or cat litter. Close glass doors or make sure a spark-arresting firescreen is covering the fireplace opening.

When you decorate the mantel, never extend decorations below the top of the mantelpiece. If you choose to hang garlands or Christmas stockings from the mantel, don't light a wood fire while the decorations are in place.

Insurance issues

For the most part, an existing fireplace in a home is covered by homeowners insurance policies. The exception may be a freestanding fireplace, such as a wood-burning stove. If you move into a home with a wood-burning stove or add one after you move in, an insurance representative may need to come to your home to inspect the unit. Your insurance company can also supply you with safety information about installing and using fireplaces and stoves.

Check your insurance policy for coverage regarding the chimney. Inspections and cleaning may be considered basic home maintenance and may not be covered.

Owner's manual

When you purchase a fireplace or stove, be sure to read the owner's manual and keep it handy. Every model is a bit different, and you'd be wise to know the particulars for safe and efficient operation. If the manual is misplaced, check the manufacturer's website for a downloadable or mail-order copy, or contact your dealer for a replacement.

Labels and seals

Every new fireplace or stove must have a Consumer Product Safety Commission (CPSC) label that gives you information about where to place the unit and how to use it. However, this label does not ensure that the unit has been tested for safety. Nationally recognized testing laboratories for wood-burning units are:

- Omni Environmental Services, Solid Fuel Testing Laboratory
- PFS Corporation
- Underwriters Laboratories, Inc.
- Underwriters Laboratories of Canada, Inc.
- Warnock Hersey International, Inc.

When buying a wood-burning unit, look for a seal from one of these sources to ensure that the unit meets minimum industry-accepted safety standards.

Governing agencies

The standard-bearer of installation requirements for solid-fuel burning devices—which includes wood-burning fireplaces and stoves—is the National Fire Protection Association (NFPA). Visit its website at *nfpa.org*. Nearly all manufacturers design their products to meet NFPA specifications. Ask the dealer about NFPA compliance before you buy a fireplace or stove and be sure the unit is installed to this standard.

The Environmental Protection Agency (EPA) also imposes strict requirements regarding energy efficiency and particle emissions. All wood stoves sold in the United States require EPA certification, but wood-burning fireplaces in some municipalities do not have to meet these requirements. For more information, visit the EPA website at *epa.gov*.

When shopping for a new gas fireplace, be sure it is lab-certified by an organization that is accepted by your local codes, such as the American Gas Association (AGA). Again, be sure the unit is installed to this standard.

Inspection & Repair

Just as you need an annual physical, your fireplace and chimney need a thorough checkup every year before the heating season begins.

Chimney inspection

Inspect your chimney once a year. Late spring or early summer is a good time, when heating season is over. If you wait until fall, the busiest time of year for fireplace installers and chimney sweeps, you may not have enough time to complete any necessary repairs before heating season begins again.

Inspecting a wood-burning fireplace yourself is not difficult, but prepare to get dirty. Wear old clothes—including a hat—and equip yourself with a dust mask or respirator and a pair of safety goggles. First, check the firebox for damage or cracks. In a masonry fireplace, also check for loose or missing bricks and mortar. Defects in a firebox usually can be repaired with refractory cement—a tough, heatproof sealant available from fireplace dealers. A damaged refractory liner in a prefabricated fireplace often can be replaced without having to replace the entire unit.

Open the damper completely. It should move freely and sit snugly against the throat. Use a powerful flashlight to look up into the throat to check the condition of the damper (*opposite, top left*. The damper should be sound with no cracks, severe pitting, or rusted-out sections. Over the years, a metal damper often will deteriorate from the water vapor and corrosive gases produced by burning wood. Broken or corroded dampers should be replaced by a professional.

Look up inside the flue and check for broken or damaged brick or defects in the flue liner. Vertical cracking in the flue liner is a telltale sign of a previous flue

fire. Any defects should be considered serious potential hazards. Consult a professional chimney sweep or masonry contractor who is familiar with fireplace repairs. Be prepared: Fixing or replacing a chimney liner is an expensive job.

Look for any obstructions such as branches, bird nests, or other debris that can restrict airflow. Finally, inspect for creosote deposits. If creosote has built up to a thickness greater than $\frac{1}{8}$ inch, it should be removed.

If you can't see the entire flue from below, you'll have to get up on the roof and inspect the flue from the top of the chimney, something that can be quite dangerous, particularly if you have a steep roof. You may wish to hire a professional chimney sweep to do this and to clean the chimney.

If you do decide to perform this inspection yourself, don't climb up onto the roof unless your roof has a pitch of 6-in-12 or less, and you are completely confident in your abilities. Do not climb onto the roof if you are alone at home. Make a safety ladder by attaching ridge hooks to the end of a ladder section. Use it by hanging the hooks over the roof ridge so the ladder lies flat and secure against the roof surface.

Cleaning the chimney

Cleaning a chimney is not beyond the abilities of any handy homeowner, but common sense should prevail. Don't work on roofs with a pitch greater than 6-in-12. Wear a respirator, safety goggles, gloves, and old clothes. Wear good-quality, rubber-soled shoes for traction. Use a

safety ladder as described above.

The safest and most effective way to clean a chimney is with a chimney brush. These are big, round or square brushes with stiff wire or polypropylene bristles and are available at fireplace retailers and home improvement centers. The brushes are attached to a long flexible rod made of fiberglass. The rods have threaded ends so that additional rod sections can be added to lengthen the brush.

The first step in chimney cleaning is to place a drop cloth in front of the fireplace to catch soot and debris. Next, seal off the front of the fireplace opening with a sheet of plastic and some duct tape. If you must tape the plastic to painted surfaces, use painter's tape.

Then, you'll need to climb to the roof, taking the chimney brush and added fiberglass lengths with you. Use a screwdriver to remove the chimney cap (*opposite, top right*). Remove the cap and then begin using the chimney brush to clean the inside of the flue (*opposite, center left*). Start with the original brush length, pushing it up and down the sides of the flue. Then screw another rod onto the brush assembly and scrub another portion. Keep working in this fashion until the entire length of the flue is scrubbed clean. When you're finished cleaning the chimney, screw the chimney cap back in place (*opposite, center right*) and return to the front of the firebox. Remove the plastic shield and clean the interior of the firebox and the smoke shelf with a heavy-duty shop vacuum. Use a scrub brush to remove any remaining debris (*opposite bottom*).

the pros know best

For ultimate peace of mind, let professionals maintain your hearth.

If you prefer to leave the messy chore of inspecting and cleaning your fireplace to someone else, hire a professional chimney sweep. Rather than just picking a name out of the phone book, ask friends and neighbors for a recommendation or check with your fireplace dealer. These retailers often keep a list of professionals with good credentials on hand.

Although the chimney sweep industry is not regulated or licensed by any government agency, many sweeps apply for certification by the Chimney Safety Institute of America (CSIA) or membership in the National Chimney Sweep Guild (NCSG). These organizations promote professionalism in the industry by testing applicants and offering continuing education on ever-changing fireplace technology and safety. For more information and to find a certified chimney sweep in your area, call the CSIA at 800/536-0118, or visit the website at *csia.org*. Visit the NCSG at *ncsg.org*.

Generally for less than $200, a sweep—such as Dan Hughes of Chiminey Cricket Family Chimney Sweeps, who showed us the many careful steps involved in cleaning a fireplace and chimney—will give your fireplace and chimney a thorough cleaning and inspection. Some sweeps lower video cameras and lights into chimneys to provide a close look at walls and liner surfaces and to establish a visual record of the chimney's condition for the homeowner. Many sweeps are qualified to complete repairs or will recommend a professional masonry contractor to do the job.

Contact your fireplace dealer for maintenance on a gas fireplace unit. The installer knows the requirements of your model and can check that all parts are working properly and are free of obstructions, and can replace any parts as well as the faux embers.

Keeping your fireplace clean is important for many reasons: safety, efficiency, and longevity. Contact your dealer for annual maintenance on your gas appliance.

Glossary

Andirons: Metal supports that sit in the firebox to hold firewood off the floor so air can circulate beneath the fire. An andiron has a horizontal metal bar with "feet" holding it up. At the front and back are upright metal bars to hold the firewood in place on the horizontal bar. Often, the front upright bars that face the room are decorative.

BTU: Abbreviation for "British thermal unit," the amount of heat needed to raise the temperature of a pound of water by 1 degree Fahrenheit. Often the amount of heat a fireplace or other appliance generates is rated in BTUs.

Chimney: The enclosure of the flue from the top of the firebox to the point where the flue ends and smoke and gases release. More commonly, however, "chimney" refers to the portion on the outside of the house, either protruding from the roof or alongside the building and over the top of the roof (see page 161).

Knowing the basic parts, operation, and terminology of a fireplace will help you to understand when problems arise and communicate your concerns to hearth industry professionals.

Corbel: A bracket, generally as deep as it is wide, that juts out from the fireplace lintel and jambs to support the weight of the mantel. Found in pairs or series (see page 5).

Cord: A measurement of firewood. A cord of wood is 128 cubic feet. For example, 4-foot lengths of wood stacked 8 feet wide and 4 feet high ($8 \times 4 \times 4 = 128$). Wood piled or sold by the cord is sometimes referred to as cordwood.

Creosote: A black or brown gooey, tarlike substance that is a byproduct of the wood-burning process. It deposits on the flue when the hot smoke and exhaust gases hit the cooler walls of the flue. Creosote is flammable, and its buildup is cause for concern. Keeping a fire burning at higher temperatures helps prevent creosote buildup.

Direct-vent: A gas-fueled fireplace that sends exhaust gases directly out of the house through a vent without a chimney. These highly efficient units don't require indoor air for combustion, which can cause loss of heat: Outdoor air enters through an inner sleeve on the same vent that exhausts air (see page 165).

Draw: The airflow in a wood-burning fireplace that pulls smoke, heat, and air up the chimney and out of the house (see page 141).

Fireback: A cast iron plate that lines the back of a wood-burning fireplace. Often decorative, these pieces protect the back of the firebox.

Fireboard: A decorative screen, often painted, placed in front of the firebox when the fireplace is not in use. A fireboard covers the "black hole" of an unused fireplace.

Firebox: The chamber in which the fire burns. Fireboxes are lined with non-combustible materials to contain the fire and are configured to direct the fumes up the chimney (see pages 5 and 141).

Firelog: An alternative fireplace fuel usually made of wood chips or shavings and wax that have been compressed into a cylindrical shape.

Firebrick: Refractory (heat-resistant) brick that lines the firebox of modern fireplaces (see page 141).

Flue: The shaft inside the chimney that runs from the top of the firebox to the top of the chimney (see page 141). The diameter, shape, and height of the flue need to be properly sized to suit the size of the fireplace to ensure proper airflow (draw).

Gas logs: An artificial log made from ceramics, refractory material, or concrete and shaped to resemble natural wood. It conceals the pipes and nozzles of a gas-burning fireplace. A gas log set gives a gas-burning fireplace the look of a wood-burning one.

Grate (also dog grate): A welded iron framework used in place of andirons to hold firewood off the hearth floor.

Hearth: Originally the word "hearth" referred only to the floor of the fireplace where the fire burns, and could include the area in front of the fireplace that's made of non-combustible material (a slate hearth, for example). Today, however, the term is often used to refer to the entire fireplace (see page 141).

Insert: Used to retrofit an existing fireplace, inserts fit inside an empty firebox to change the fuel source and improve efficiency.

Jamb: A vertical support below the lintel on either side of a fireplace opening (see page 5).

Kindling: Small pieces of dried wood that burn faster than full-size logs. Kindling is placed beneath and around the larger logs and is lit first to help ignite the larger pieces of wood.

Kiva: Constructed of adobe, these beehive-shape fireplaces have shallow, angled walls that radiate heat outward.

Lintel: A horizontal block that spans the space over a fireplace opening between the two vertical supports, or jambs (see page 5).

Mantel (or chimneypiece): A shelf over the opening of a fireplace that is purely decorative (see pages 5 and 141).

Masonry heater: Originally popular in Europe, masonry heaters are stone wrapped around a relatively small firebox. The heat from the fire is absorbed by the masonry and released gradually into the room, providing even heat.

Overmantel: The area above the mantel shelf. It is often decorated with trim or stonework elements that help define the style of the fireplace (see page 5).

Pellet stove: A type of stove designed to burn small pellets of compressed sawdust. The pellets drop into the firebox at regular intervals to maintain even heat output.

Pilaster: Vertical flat columns often found on the jambs of a wood fireplace surround. A pilaster projects only slightly and is usually made up of a base, a shaft, and a capital.

Prefabricated fireplace: Fireplaces used to be constructed "from scratch" on-site. Today, the firebox and its surrounding structure are often built in a factory, prefabricated, and shipped to the installation site. These units are made more from metal than masonry, so they're much lighter and less expensive.

Raised hearth: Building the fireplace several inches off the floor, often with a ledge for seating, to create a whole new view. Raised hearths are often used in dining rooms or other areas where furniture is likely to block the view of a fireplace at floor level (see page 5).

Rumford fireplace: Named after 18th-century scientist Count Rumford, these fireplaces are characterized by shallow fireboxes, rounded throats and sharply angled side walls. This configuration radiates much of the fire's heat into the room while efficiently drawing smoke and gases up the flue (see page 142).

Seasoned wood: For wood to burn efficiently and without creating creosote, it must be quite dry, and the drying process requires several months. For example, wood cut in the spring and allowed to dry over the summer, or a season, will be relatively dry for use the following fall or winter. Wood that has been allowed to dry for at least six months is preferred.

Slip: Area between the firebox and the surrounding casework. Usually covered with stone or tile, the slip acts as a fireproof barrier between the burning hearth and a wood surround (see page 5).

Surround: The components of the fireplace that surround the firebox below the overmantel. This is usually comprised of a slip, jambs, lintel, and mantel (see pages 5 and 141).

Vent-free: By sealing a gas-burning fireplace and creating a super-efficient firebox, a fireplace can burn safely without venting to the outdoors. These units do still produce exhaust gases, so some communities have restrictions about where vent-free fireplaces can be installed (see page 173).

Zero-clearance: A prefab fireplace designed to be safely installed very close to wood wall studs and other combustible materials.

Resources

Fireplace Manufacturers

Austroflamm
011/43-7249-46443-0; *austroflamm.com*
Austrian manufacturer of Euro-style wood and gas stoves.

Buckley Rumford Fireplaces
360/385-9974; *rumford.com*
Maker of Rumford-type fireplaces.

Dimplex North America
800/668-6663; *dimplex.com*
Manufacturer of electric fireplaces and stoves for the ambiance of a fire with no venting.

FMI Products, LLC
800/432-5212; *fmifireplace.com*
Manufacturer of wood-burning, gas-burning, vented, and vent-free fireplaces.

FireOrb
847/454-9198; *fireorb.net*
Manufacturer of an oval, suspended metal fireplace with a 360-degree rotation field.

Hearth & Home Technologies
800/926-4356; *hearthnhome.com*, *quadrafire.com*
Maker of Quadrafire, Heat-N-Glow, and Heatilator fireplaces.

HearthStone Quality Home Heating Products
800/827-8603
hearthstonestoves.com
Producer of handmade soapstone wood-burning and gas stoves; each stove is signed by the craftsperson who made it.

Jøtul
207/797-5912; *jotulflame.com*
Manufacturer of cast iron, wood- and gas-burning stoves, inserts, and fireplaces.

Kozy Heat
800/253-4904; *kozyheat.com*
Manufacturer of indoor and outdoor gas-burning fireplaces. Also offers a wood-burning unit that can be converted to gas.

Lennox Hearth Products
360/757-9728; *lennoxhearthproducts.com*, *whitfield.com*
Manufacturer of pellet and gas stoves and inserts. Brands include Whitfield pellet stoves and Lennox fireplaces and freestanding stoves.

Majestic Fireplaces
800/525-1989; *majesticproducts.com*
A division of CFM Specialty Home Products, manufacturer of a large selection of gas fireplaces, stoves, and inserts.

Malm
800/535-8955; *malmfireplaces.com*
Manufacturer of gas- and wood-burning fireplaces and the FireFlame wood-burning fireplace-barbecue grill. Also custom designs fireplaces.

Pacific Energy
250/748-1184; *pacificenergy.net*
Manufacturer of wood and gas stoves and inserts.

Rais & Wittus, Inc.
914/764-5679; *raiswittus.com*
U.S. distributor of RAIS Euro-style gas- and wood-burning high-efficiency fireplaces and stoves.

Real Flame
800/654-1704; *realflame.com*
Manufacturer of gel fuels, gel-burning fireplace units, mantels, and accessories.

Regency Fireplace Products
regency-fire.com; Manufacturer of wood and gas fireplaces, stoves, and inserts.

Robert H. Peterson Company
rhpeterson.co
Manufacturer of gas logs.

RSF Woodburning Fireplaces
450/565-6336; *icc-rsf.com*
Manufacturer specializing in high-tech, high-efficiency, clean-burning wood hearth products.

Thelin Hearth Products
800/949-5048; *thelinco.com*
Manufacturer of pellet and gas stoves with an old-time look.

Travis Industries, Inc.
800/654-1177; *travisproducts.com*
Manufacturer of Lopi brand wood, pellet, and gas stoves and fireplace inserts; Fireplace Xtraordinair wood and gas fireplaces and inserts; and Avalon wood, pellet, and gas stoves and inserts.

Tulikivi U.S., Inc.
tulikivi.com
Tulikivi is Finnish for "fire stone." The company makes wood-burning soapstone fireplaces that cleanly and efficiently absorb and radiate heat into the room.

Vermont Castings
800/525-1898; *vermontcastings.com*
A division of CFM Specialty Home Products, maker of a large selection of gas fireplaces, stoves, and inserts.

Virtual Fireplaces
virtualproducts.com
Makes high-definition monitors that fit into an existing fireplace cavity or into new construction to provide the image and sound of a wood-burning fire.

Wilkening Fireplace Co.
800/367-7976
hearth.com/wilkening/info.html
Manufacturer of high-efficiency wood-burning fireplaces featuring the Ultimate Seal Airtight door, including the Intens-A-Fyre, Ultra Great, and Magna-Fyre.

Woodstock Soapstone Co., Inc.
800/866-4344; *woodstocksoapstone.com*
Handmade wood- and gas-burning stoves, including a catalytic wood stove with the even, radiant heat of soapstone.

Mantel & Surround Suppliers

A+ Woodworking
864/836-2918; *custommantels.com*
Manufacturer of custom mantels, shelves, and mantel ornaments.

Architectural Salvage Warehouse
802/658-5011; *architecturalsalvagevt.com*
Antiques warehouse carrying salvaged mantels.

Carolina Architectural Salvage
803/337-3939; *cogansantiques.com*
Salvaged hearth items.

Collinswood Designs
970/482-3610; *collinswooddesigns.com*
Shelves, surrounds, related cabinetry, overmantels.

Distinctive Mantel Designs Inc.
303/592-7474; *distinctivemantels.com*
Maker of wood and cast-stone mantels.

Elegance in Stone
eleganceinstone.com
Fireplace surrounds of granite, marble, and limestone.

Foster Mantel
800/285-8551; *mantels.net*
Handcrafted mantels, shelves, and caps.

Grand Mantel, Inc.
866/473-9663; *grandmantel.com*
Maker of artisan-crafted hardwood mantel cabinetry.

Mantels of Yesteryear
888/292-2080; *mantelsofyesteryear.com*
Manufacturer of late-1700s- to early-1900s-style reproduction mantels.

Salvage One
312/733-0098; *salvageone.com*
Architectural salvage warehouse that sells surrounds, mantels, and firebacks.

West End Architectural Salvage
515/243-4405; *westendsalvage.com*
Four-story architectural salvage warehouse that sells surrounds, mantels, and overmantels.

Associations

Chimney Safety Institute of America
800/536-0118; *csia.org*
Find CSIA-certified sweeps in your area.

Hearth Education Foundation
703/524-8030; *heartheducation.org*
Use the website to find local HEF-certified professionals.

Hearth, Patio, & Barbecue Association
703/522-0086; *hpba.org*
The Hearth, Patio & Barbecue Association brings timely and useful information to consumers who use or are considering the purchase of hearth, patio or barbecue products.

Masonry Heater Association of North America
802/728-5896; *mha-net.org*
Use the website to find a local certified heater mason.

National Chimney Sweep Guild
ncsg.org
Also see listing for Chimney Safety Institute of America.

National Fire Protection Association
800/344-3555; *nfpa.org*
Organization provides helpful consumer safety information.

Pellet Fuels Institute
703/522-6778; *pelletheat.org*
The non-profit Institute educates consumers about using wood pellet fuel.

Makeover Resources

Pages 136-139: Cane Chairs, 2.70002; Flying wall bowls, pale aqua 8.81280 — **Global Views;** *globalviews.com;* 888/956-0030. Zuma Iron/Brass Convex Mirror, Sabre Mahogany Veneer and Solids accent table, Dalton Satin Brass floor lamp—**Arteriors Home;** *arteriorshome.com;* 877/488-8866. Proky Hefer Wooden Pendant A, B & C; Gemma Orkin Bird silk pillow cover; Gemma Orkin Wildflower silk pillow cover; Allegra Hicks Kaleidoscope pillow cover; Favorite throw, sky—**West Elm;** *westelm.com;* 888/922-4119. Market Baskets/set of 3—**Ballard Designs;** *ballarddesigns.com;* 800/536-7551. Waving Grass flat fireplace screen in bronze, Nate Berkus Snakeskin decorative pillow—**Target;** *target.com.* Silk Dupioni curtain panels—**Antique Drapery Rod Co.;** *antiquedraperyrod.com;* 214/653-1733. Labyrinth Lake Rug—**Company C;** companyc.com; 800/818-8288. Artwork—**Tandem Brick;** *tandembrick.com;* 515/282-103

Pages 174-175: Trend Stone granite overlay in Sachi— **Granite Transformations;** *granitetransformations.com.* Victory direct-vent insert—**Vermont Castings;** *vermontcastings.com.* Golden Wheat, Terra Cotta and Sea Green Medallion Soumak Rug—**Shades of Light;** *shadesoflight.com;* 800/262-6612.

Product photos courtesy of **Hampton,** page 161 (bottom left); **Lowe's,** page 143 (bottom left), page 172 (left), page 173 (top), page 179 (top left and bottom left; **Monessen,** page 143 (top right), page 165 (bottom); **Overstock,** page 143 (bottom right), page 172 (top right); **Regency,** page 143 (top left), page 160 (bottom), page 161 (top left), page 162, page 163, page 164 (bottom), page 172 (bottom right).

Index

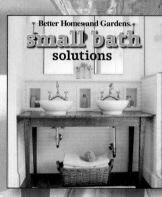